# Accounting &Financial Management

## *for Residential Construction*

**Fifth Edition**

# EMMA SHINN

**BuilderBooks.com®**

BOOKS THAT BUILD YOUR BUSINESS

A Service of
**NAHB**
NATIONAL ASSOCIATION
OF HOME BUILDERS

# Accounting and Financial Management, 5th Edition
## Emma Shinn

BuilderBooks.com®, a Service of the National Association of Home Builders

| | |
|---|---|
| Courtenay S. Brown | Director, Book Publishing |
| Doris M. Tennyson | Senior Editor |
| Natalie Holms | Book Editor |
| Torrie Singletary | Production Editor |
| Open Soul Design | Cover Design |
| Pine Tree Composition | Composition |
| Hamilton Printing | Printing |

| | |
|---|---|
| Gerald M. Howard | NAHB Executive Vice President and CEO |
| Mark Pursell | NAHB Senior Staff Vice President, Marketing & Sales Group |
| Lakisha Campbell | NAHB Staff Vice President, Publication & Affinity Programs |

## Disclaimer

This publication provides accurate information on the subject matter covered. The publisher is selling it with the understanding that the publisher is not providing legal, accounting, or other professional service. If you need legal advice or other expert assistance, you should obtain the services of a qualified professional experienced in the subject matter involved. Reference herein to any specific commercial products, process, or service by trade name, trademark, manufacturer, or otherwise, does not necessarily constitute or imply its endorsement, recommendation, or favored status by the National Association of Home Builders. The views and opinions of the author expressed in this publication do not necessarily state or reflect those of the National Association of Home Builders, and they shall not be used to advertise or endorse a product.

Printed in the United States of America

10  09  08          1   2   3   4   5

ISBN-978-0-86718-635-2

Library of Congress Cataloging-in-Publication Data

Shinn, Emma S.
  Accounting and financial management for residential construction / Emma Shinn. -- 5th ed.
    p. cm.
  Includes index.
  ISBN 978-0-86718-635-2
  1. Construction industry--United States--Accounting. 2. Managerial accounting--United States. I. Title.
  HF5686.B7S54 2008
  657'.869--dc22

                                                                                            2008004190

For further information, please contact:

National Association of Home Builders
1201 15th Street, NW
Washington, DC 20005-2800
800-223-2665
Visit us online at www.BuilderBooks.com®.

# Contents

# List of Illustrations

# About the Author

Emma Shinn, CPA, is an officer of the Shinn Group of Companies, including the Lee Evans Group, Shinn Consulting, and Builder Partnerships in Littleton, Colorado. In the 1960s, she worked for Touche, Ross and Company (now Delotte & Touche). She has an MBA in accounting from The American University in Washington, D.C., and is a certified public accountant (CPA). She served as Chairman of the NAHB Business Management and Information Technology Committee in 1997.

Her background in the industry includes all aspects of the building process including planning, design, supervision, sales and administration of single-family projects. She received the MAME Award for the Rookie Salesperson of the Year presented by the Denver Home Builders Association in 1988. Emma's specialization is accounting for the home building industry, addressing not only financial reporting but also the use of accounting information in the management process.

# Acknowledgments

This fifth edition of *Accounting and Financial Management for Residential Construction* is the product of several years of planning, writing, and reviewing by people working to improve the management of home building, remodeling, and land development firms.

Special credit is due to Lee S. Evans, retired, Nederland, Colorado, who developed the original NAHB Chart of Accounts. The NAHB Financial Management Issues Work Group of the Business Management & Information Technology Committee has updated the chart of accounts again for this fifth edition.

Many thanks to the following individuals who contributed their expertise and time to reviewing the manuscript for this fifth edition of *Accounting and Financial Management for Residential Construction*: Anita Deen, Administrative Manager, The Shinn Group, Littleton, Colorado; Steve Hays, Partner, Rubin Brown, St. Louis Missouri; Craig Schweikart, Vice President, Builder 360, Constellation HomeBuilder Systems Inc., Redmond, Washington; and Charles C. Shinn, Jr., President, The Shinn Group, Littleton, Colorado.

The author thanks the following individuals who reviewed the previous editions: Greg Caruso, President, Caruso Homes, Crofton Maryland; Steve Maltzman, President, SMA Consulting, Redlands, California; Ken Waetzman, President, Waetzman Realty Advisors, Cherry Hill, New Jersey; and Jamie Wolf, President, Wolfworks, Farmington, Connecticut.

# Introduction

E very company should produce monthly financial statements and other reports for management use. Just as any home or building must rest on a secure and solid foundation, an understanding of accounting should be the firm foundation upon which a company rests.

This revised and expanded fifth edition of *Accounting and Financial Management for Residential Construction* assumes the reader has no previous knowledge of accounting. It uses straightforward and easy-to-comprehend explanations and illustrations to help builders, remodelers, and developers understand accounting and bookkeeping terminology and procedures.

Emma Shinn will lead the reader through the process in a methodical manner, building concept upon concept so that even the most complex accounting functions can be easily understood.

This book can be used by any type of builder (single-family, multifamily, or commercial), remodeler, and developer. It includes the complete, updated NAHB Chart of Accounts (to be adapted to your business) and the job cost control subsidiary ledger accounts for direct, indirect, and land development costs.

This fifth edition of *Accounting and Financial Management*

- presents an overview of accounting and how an accounting system operates
- offers guidelines and a general structure for designing an accounting system
- presents general concepts and principles of financial planning and analysis
- details how to integrate job cost accounting with estimating, purchasing, and scheduling
- explains how technology facilitates accounting processes
- explains how owners and managers can use financial reporting to enhance and improve their companies
- provides special tips for multiple-project builders (Chapter 11), developers (Chapter 12), and remodelers (Chapter 13) to use and benefit from the profit center concept

Although the book begins with the basics, readers can go as deeply as they wish. In fact, some builders, remodelers, and developers give the book to their certified public accountants (CPAs) with their records at year's end to facilitate the CPA's understanding of the unique aspects of residential construction and remodeling.

Moreover, using financial reporting systems helps builders, remodelers, and developers determine their financial position at any time; compare current and historical performance; and benchmark their performance against other builders, remodelers, developers; and even the industry itself.

So, roll up your sleeves, grab your financial data, a cup of coffee, and get started.

# CHAPTER 1

# Designing the System and Choosing an Accountant

Accounting is one of the most powerful management tools available to owners and managers of home building companies, but it is also the most undervalued and underutilized: a number of owners and managers consider it a necessary evil.

Traditionally, the purpose of accounting for home builders has been to report to third parties: lenders, the Internal Revenue Service (IRS), and other taxing authorities. Accounting training also has focused primarily on third-party reporting responsibilities rather than reporting to managers or internal users. It does so understandably because of the seriousness of the professional liability for submitting erroneous information to third parties. For example, third parties rely on financial reports to make investment decisions. Therefore, if the reports are inaccurate, investors can sustain unanticipated personal losses.

As end users, neither the lenders nor the investors need as much detail in financial reporting as company owners. In fact, these users prefer to have financial transactions classified in broad categories to facilitate an aerial view rather than a close up of a company's operations and finances. Unlike company owners, lenders and investors want to evaluate the profitability and financial strength of the business, not analyze where profits come from or what functions they could improve to increase profits. Therefore, emphasizing third-party reporting risks neglecting accounting's role as a management tool.

This book introduces the reader to an even more important purpose for accounting than third-party reporting—facilitating and enhancing company management. Every accounting system requires the user to record financial transactions in chronological sequence to document historical events. During the process a firm accumulates a wealth of information about the business that could easily enhance the ability of the managers to make sound decisions.

The accounting system holds large amounts of data as it measures each economic activity that takes place in the company. It is the lifeblood of the company because it touches every department and function. At no additional expense, it can provide managers at every level with critical information to improve each function or department of the company. Yet, this system is probably the most overlooked and underutilized source of information in a home building company. From this book, you will learn accounting from the basics up and how to use it to meet your individual needs.

## What Is Accounting?

Accounting is the process of collecting, classifying, and accumulating historical financial transactions in categories and reports that will accurately reflect operational performance (income statement) and the present financial position (balance sheet). Owners and managers should organize the accounting system so that it can produce the types of reports and level of detail needed for managing the company effectively. How the system is set up will impact the types of reports and the amount of detail present in the reports.

The accounting system should be designed as a *management system* to meet management needs not solely as a system to comply with third party reporting requirements. You can easily use a system designed to meet management needs to meet the requirements of third-party users. However, the reverse is not true: it is time-consuming and, in some instances, almost impossible, to prepare detailed management reports from a system set up primarily to support tax and third-party requirements.

A well-organized accounting function allows owners and managers to obtain financial reports that make business decisions less of a guessing game. A strong system will help you estimate the cost of future jobs, set goals, and objectives, prepare short- and long-term budgets. In addition, historical financial data in accounting records help owners and managers with the following three tasks:

1. Measurement
   - actual performance
   - the results of functions or departments
   - profitability and problem situations
2. Analysis
   - past performance
   - trends
3. Evaluation
   - financial strength of the company
   - feasibility of future projects
   - growth goals

Accounting provides the framework for the company's control system. It enables comparisons of actual performance to goals and objectives in quantitative and financial terms. This practice allows easy comparison between the plan and the actual performance: the essence of any control system.

Before proceeding, review the five basic management functions: planning, organizing, staffing, directing, and controlling. The following paragraphs describe these functions.

*Planning* sets the stage for profitability. The company develops a road map to direct the diverse resources of the company toward an established goal in a particular time period. The plan includes targets, objectives, and benchmarks against which the company will measure its performance.

*Organizing* structures the company for profitability. It orchestrates the company's diverse resources to focus on the objectives and accomplish the work required to implement the company's plans and achieve its goals.

*Staffing* requires hiring and training for profitability. The company must hire qualified people as well as continually train its workforce.

*Directing* leads the staff to profitability. It requires supervising the workforce and monitoring the company's resources to ensure they are used efficiently to accomplish the plans and objectives.

*Controlling* "compels events to conform to the plan," Lee S. Evans.[1]

Company officials use the resulting analysis to measure performance and compare it with the plan. They use the resulting analysis to redirect resources, if necessary, to accomplish the goals and objectives.

As a management tool, accounting plays a key role in both planning and controlling. Savvy builders, remodelers, and developers recognize the positive impact of using accounting information to manage their companies. With reliable accounting systems, owners and managers can

- make decisions based on facts, not just gut feelings
- know where the company stands at any moment and eliminate year-end surprises
- make informed decisions about allocating resources to new ventures
- have time to react to adverse conditions
- measure the performance of each function or department of the company, including construction, financing, sales and marketing, and general administration
- measure the performance of each community or project
- create a historical record and a road map for future planning and budgeting
- collect and maintain documentation for loan applications and prospectuses for potential investors
- strengthen negotiations with vendors and trade contractors by using records of previous activity
- provide staff members with objective information to help them (and you) eliminate waste, variances, and other inefficiencies

Therefore, don't underestimate the power of accounting in day-to-day operations management. In addition to the traditional set of financial statements you prepare to satisfy lenders and governmental requirements (balance sheet and income statement), a well-designed accounting system can produce reports to facilitate and enhance the effectiveness of the management process.

---

1. Lee S. Evans was a management educator and consultant to the home building industry from 1954–92. He is the only educator honored by induction into the NAHB Hall of Fame and as one of *Builder* magazine's 100 American Housing's Most Influential Leaders in the Last Century in 1999.

## Designing the System

Like a house, remodeling job, or new subdivision, a successful accounting system starts with sound design. Pay special attention to the following two steps:

First, identify whether the company functions as a sole proprietorship, partnership, C or S corporation, or limited liability corporation (LLC). Reporting requirements and the accounts required to track the ownership interest differ under each type of entity. In addition, the size and the organizational structure impact the types of reports the company needs to generate. As a result, accounting systems become more complex for large organizations than for small companies.

Second, analyze all functions and departments, such as field operations, sales and marketing, financing, estimating and purchasing, and warranty and customer service. Determine who is responsible for each function. Prepare an organizational chart that shows every function in a hierarchy and includes the names of employees responsible for carrying out each function (fig. 1.1).

In a small company, one individual may be responsible for more than one function. In large companies, each function may need to be broken down into subfunctions, with each staffed by a different employee. These companies often need more accounts to classify and track financial transactions.

Of course, many small companies aim to grow over time. Therefore, prepare for expansion and growth with the following steps:

- Project future growth and determine its effect on resources and staff as well as production volume. Identify future staffing requirements and when and where you will need new employees. Revise the organizational chart to incorporate new positions (fig. 1.2). Make projections carefully because company size impacts the accounting system's design, including the type of reports to be produced and the controls needed.

- Identify the reports you want the system to generate. As you design reports, determine their relevancy, frequency, users, and level detail required. Once your system has been designed, major revisions to reports might require changes in the system's basic structure and disrupt the existing system's capabilities during implementation of the changes.

Under no circumstances should an accountant or consultant design an accounting system without the active participation of the builder, remodeler, or developer. For large companies, the top management team needs to participate in the design process. With the owners and managers actively participating in its design, the system will be more likely to satisfy the company's needs.

**Figure 1.1** Small-volume organizational chart

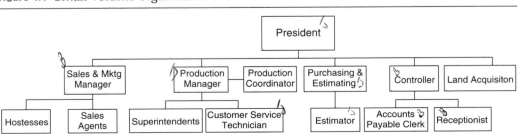

**Figure 1.2** Medium- to large-volume organizational chart

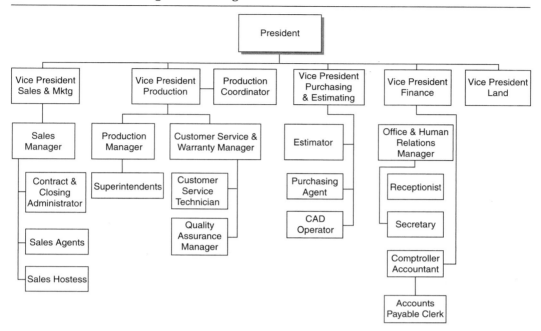

Beware when purchasing a computer software package. While it may provide the mechanism to process transactions, an off-the-shelf program may not meet your management needs. However, off-the-shelf systems can and should be customized.

## Choosing an Accountant

An accounting system requires attention on both the professional and technical levels. Certified public accountants (CPAs) and accountants provide the professional input; whereas bookkeepers and clerical personnel manage the technical aspects such as the data entry and processing. The difference between accountants and CPAs is primarily in their approach and who they work for.

CPA is a professional designation with high educational and ethical requirements. As a member of an independent accounting firm, a CPA is primarily concerned with the accuracy of the financial statements as prepared by a company. The CPA audits, reviews, or compiles the financial statements, and for audits, they can verify to third parties the statements' accuracy or lack of it.

In contrast, while an accountant may also have CPA credentials, he or she is usually a company employee. The accountant maintains internal controls, prepares financial statements and management reports, and helps analyze the reports. Bear in mind that the financial function (reporting to third parties) and the managerial function (reporting to managers) of accounting are not in conflict. In fact, many CPA firms today offer their clients both consulting services.

CPAs use universal principles and standards as established by the American Institute of Certified Public Accountants (AICPA) board, commonly known as

Generally Accepted Accounting Principles (GAAP). They determine whether a company's financial statements fairly represent its financial position. For this purpose, CPAs require little specialized knowledge from industry to industry.

In contrast, processing and evaluating financial information for company managers requires in-depth knowledge of an industry. Therefore, not all CPA firms can provide the expertise needed to design and implement a system that will serve well both the external reporting and the management functions of a home building, remodeling, or land development company.

Consider job, development, and indirect construction costs as well as the treatment of land. For example, because at least 50% of the charges against sales revenue are construction costs, they represent the biggest single line item affecting the company's profitability. Using a job cost system that operates as a subsidiary of the general accounting system, builders can track cost by unit of production and by cost code (lumber, plumbing, electric) within each unit. This subsidiary system establishes the framework for controlling construction cost. (The *unit* is a house for the home builder, a remodeling job for the remodeler, a subdivision or community for a developer, and a commercial establishment for a light commercial builder.)

Similarly land, development costs, and indirect construction costs (including capitalization of interest) unique to the building industry require special attention from builders, remodelers, and developers. Refer to Chapter 7 for details on how to do the allocation.

Although your primary consideration should be management use of financial information, you must also pay attention to IRS regulations to ensure that the system accumulates and classifies data for easy retrieval for tax purposes at year's end. Otherwise, you might need time-consuming analysis and research to extract the required information. Because regulations change often, both you and your accountant must have a general understanding of the current regulations. For more complex tax issues, enlist the services of a tax professional. Don't try to handle them yourself.

## The Bookkeeper

Generally, bookkeepers and clerical personnel collect and classify financial information within a framework the accountant designs. The bookkeeper's job is to collect, enter, and process data. A well-trained secretary or bookkeeper can handle daily records of financial information. You also can outsource this work to a bookkeeping service or the bookkeeping division of a CPAs office. In some small-volume companies, the builder, remodeler, developer, or an office manager may perform the bookkeeping duties.

The accountant retains the responsibility for reviewing the data collection process, reviewing the data for accuracy, analyzing it, and preparing reports.

If you need to use an outside bookkeeping service, choose one that is familiar with home building, remodeling, or development. In addition, the bookkeeping service should follow the system and requirements designed for your business by an accountant familiar with home building rather than use its own generalized system. The accountant should perform a monthly or, at minimum, a quarterly review of the bookkeeping function to ensure accuracy and reliability.

## The Accountant

Selecting an accountant is a critical task for management, particularly the selection of one familiar with home building, remodeling, or land development. Because of the special requirements of each business, look for **an** accountant with experience in your line of work. For example, job cost accounting must be integrated into your system. Other unique features such as indirect construction costs will vary according to whether you operate a home building, remodeling, or development company. The accountant needs to understand your business as well as your company's management needs. When you are considering accountants, request references from other builders, remodelers, or developers who have used, or are using, them. Attorneys often can refer you to qualified accountants as well.

Finding an accounting specialist in a large town may be easier than in a small one. Present a copy of this book to your accountant as a guide to the specific requirements of the home building, remodeling, and land development industries. And as soon as company size and income permit doing so, hire an in-house accountant.

## The Certified Public Accountant

For many small companies, an in-house accountant either is not a practical option or is simply not necessary. In those cases, selecting the right CPA is critical. The CPA should not only satisfy all traditional external requirements for reporting, but he or she also should help management analyze financial information to better control the business and make educated business decisions. The CPA must understand home building in-depth (not just construction), as well as know the structure and organization of the individual company, its products and services, and construction methods.

Above all, the right CPA can make the difference between a business that merely functions and one that prospers. The owner-CPA relationship is reciprocal. Builders, remodelers, and developers must educate their CPAs in the internal operations of their companies; and in turn, the owner, managers, and staff must be receptive to the recommendations and suggestions made by the CPA. A two-way dialogue is essential to the relationship between the builder, remodeler, or developer and the CPA. Some companies use the CPA's services of only for taxes. However, others engage CPAs for audits, reviews, or compilations of accounting data. The scope of the work done by a CPA firm determines the type of service and the cost of the work performed.

### Audit

An audit is by far the most comprehensive and expensive of the services offered by a CPA firm. After an audit, the CPA firm will issue an opinion about whether the company's financial statements fairly represent the company's financial position in accordance with GAAP. The audit process takes the following actions for the appropriate third parties:

■ verifies the account balances on the balance sheet (by confirming such items as the amount of cash held in bank accounts, outstanding receivables, accounts payable, customer deposits, and loans payable)

- verifies other account balances such as inventories of materials, lots, and work-in-process through physical observation
- scrutinizes the system of internal control to ensure the existence of, and compliance with, rules and procedures

Although, typically, lenders do not require audited statements from small- or midsize companies, investors and lenders often require audits as a condition for loan approvals or capital investment.

### Reviews

Because an audit is relatively expensive, companies not required by third parties to have audits often choose a less comprehensive service, such as a review. A review provides a limited analysis or testing of the financial transactions and account balances. It generally does not include confirmation of account balances by third parties other than verification of cash balances through bank statements. Therefore, the opinion expressed after a review is limited in scope.

Many lenders require borrowers to provide annual statements that have been reviewed by a CPA firm. Because of the reduced scope of work, a review costs less than an audit. A review provides the company's owners with limited assurance that the accounting department is following accepted procedures in recording and reporting financial data.

### Compilation

A compilation is by far the least expensive of the three services offered by CPA firms. In a compilation, the CPA is under no obligation to review or investigate any account or procedure unless something looks suspicious or appears to be misleading. The CPA issues no opinion as to the accuracy of the data. The CPA simply presents the data supplied by management in an accepted financial format for disclosure to lenders, for income tax purposes, or for any other use intended by the owner.

Regardless of the service performed by the CPA, the financial statements are representations made by the home building, remodeling, or development company. Ultimately, the company, not the CPA, is responsible for accurate preparation of the financial statements.

# CHAPTER 2

# Basics of Accounting

T his chapter eliminates some of the mystery surrounding accounting for the non-accountant. Understanding the mechanics of accounting and the information well-designed management reports provide will improve your business management.

## Accounting Systems

Financial data generated by a builder, remodeler, or developer's business operations should be classified, accumulated, and summarized following GAAP. Accounting systems generally have two focuses: financial and managerial. The financial structure, or main system, provides the "big picture" (fig. 2.1). The managerial structure, or subsystem, classifies the same financial data in greater detail for use in control and decision-making.

### Financial Accounting System
The financial system maintains an overview of all financial transactions. The accountant uses it to prepare traditional financial statements, the income statement, and the balance sheet.

Accounting systems classify financial transactions into the following categories or types of accounts:

- assets
- liabilities
- owners' equity
- revenues
- expenses

*Assets* are items of value that the company owns, either tangible or intangible. Tangible assets include cash; inventories (land, work in progress, materials); office equipment; and construction equipment. Intangible assets include accounts receivable, prepaid expenses, and land deposits.

**Figure 2.1**  Nature, structure, and output of an accounting system

|  | **Main System<br>Financial Accounting** | **Subsystem<br>Managerial Accounting** |
|---|---|---|
| **Nature** | General | Detailed |
| **Structure** | Journals & general ledger | Subsidiary ledgers |
| **Output** | Financial statement:<br>    Income statement<br>    Balance sheet | Management reports:<br>    Job cost reports<br>    Gross profit reports |

*Liabilities* are obligations the company owes to third parties, such as accounts payable, construction loan payments, other loans payable, and taxes. Until the house is delivered to the buyer, customer deposits are also a liability. The builder owes the buyer either the money back or the delivery of the home.

*Owners' equity* represents the owner's interest in the company. This category, not only measures the owner's investment in the company, but also company profits the owners have chosen to reinvest in the company for growth and stability. If the company incurs losses, the owners' equity will decrease. The owners absorb these losses.

*Revenue accounts* accumulate cash from sales made by the company, whether for houses, remodeling jobs, or finished lots. Companies also earn revenues from interest and investment returns. The accounting system should classify revenue by type and identify the source of the money.

*Expenses* include the costs of the product or services sold and the costs of operating the business. Accumulating expenses in major categories helps owners analyze how dollars were spent on land or lots, direct construction costs, indirect construction costs (field expenses), financing expenses, sales and marketing expenses, and general and administrative expenses.

### Managerial Accounting System

A number of subsystems, also known as subsidiary ledgers or detailed ledger systems, comprise the managerial accounting system. Such a system could include the following subsidiary ledgers:

- material inventory
- job cost for land development
- job cost for work in progress
- finished lots
- accounts receivable
- accounts payable
- customer deposits
- construction loans payable

Figure 2.2 illustrates how accounting data flows through the system, the relationship between financial and managerial accounting, and the output generated by each. Each subsidiary ledger in the managerial accounting system contains a detailed breakdown of an account in the general ledger or financial accounting system.

The accounts payable account in the general ledger serves as a control account. It shows, in one lump sum, the amount owed to *all* suppliers, trade contractors, and others. The accounts payable subsidiary shows amounts currently owed to *each* supplier, trade contractor, and others. The total of all individual accounts in the accounts payable subsidiary ledger must equal the balance in the accounts payable account in the general ledger. This critical number validates the integrity and accuracy of the accounting information.

In the NAHB Chart of Accounts, the general ledger account (1430 direct construction cost account or work-in-progress account) supports the subsidiary account. As with accounts payable, the general ledger's direct construction account shows no detail or costs. The job cost subsidiary ledger shows not only the cost of each unit under construction, it also breaks down the costs associated with each unit.

**Figure 2.2**  Flow of data through the system

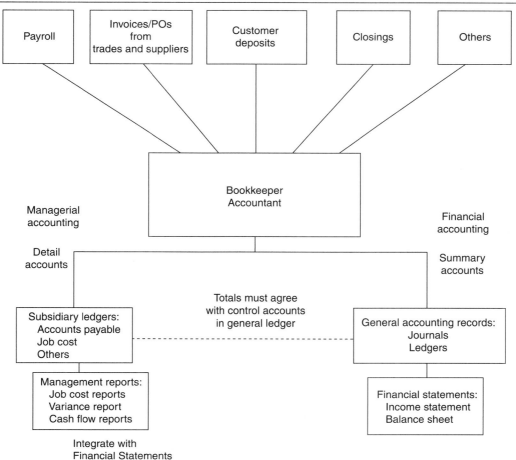

**Figure 2.3** Purchase of construction materials on account

A home builder purchased materials on account from XYZ Lumber Company to be used in house number 15. The bookkeeper records the financial information in the following places:

- the general ledger, under direct construction cost and accounts payable
- the accounts payable subsidiary, under the XYZ Lumber Company account
- the job cost subsidiary, under job number 15, in the lumber cost code

Again, to maintain the integrity of the system, the total of all units in the job cost subsidiary must equal the balance of the direct construction cost account in the general ledger (fig. 2.3). A discrepancy between the general and the subsidiary ledgers indicates errors in entering and processing transactions.

The general ledger entry indicates that the builder bought material on credit to construct a house, the accounts payable subsidiary shows how much the builder owed XYZ Lumber Company for the material, and the job cost subsidiary shows the cost of lumber used in house number 15. Remember that the total of all individual accounts in a subsidiary ledger must agree with the balance in the general ledger account.

A remodeler or developer follows the same procedure for materials he or she purchases. However, instead of using the direct construction cost account, the remodeler uses the direct cost of remodeling account. The subsidiary ledger identifies the job for which the materials were used by a job number assigned at the start of each job. The developer uses the land development cost account and identifies the specific subdivision by a given number.

Using computers for data processing does not guarantee that the subsidiary ledgers and general ledger control accounts will balance. Although some systems have safeguards to help the data entry clerk maintain the equality between the two systems, other software programs have no safeguards. Therefore, the accountant must set up processes and procedures to (1) ensure that the subsidiaries and the general ledger accounts stay in balance and (2) continually verify equality between the control account and the subsidiary.

Managers must be able to trust the financial information generated by the accounting system if they are going to use it as a management tool and use the accounting reports to make important decisions. If the numbers are not reliable, managers will resist basing decisions on them. Moreover, once management loses confidence in the accounting information, regaining that trust is difficult.

## Accounting Equation

The general accounting system rests on the following equation:

$$\text{Assets} = \text{Equities}$$

*Assets* represent items of value the company owns, such as cash, inventories, furniture, and equipment; and *equities* represent the source of capital (either from the owners, creditors, or lenders) used to acquire the assets. Thus, the equity side of the equation may be expressed as follows:

Equities = Liabilities (debt) + Owners' equity (investment)

Businesspeople often refer to accounting as a double-entry system. Such a system requires that every financial transaction be recorded in at least two accounts. For example, a person decides to open a home building business. After the owner sets up the appropriate business structure (sole proprietorship, partnership, limited liability corporation [LLC], or other corporation), the owner deposits $200,000 in his or her new business account.

The accounting entry to record this transaction requires that cash be recorded in the cash account (on the asset side of the equation) and that the investment be recorded in owner's equity (on the equity side) in the following manner:

Assets = Equities

Cash $200,000 = Owner's Equity $200,000

The accounting equation follows the same principles of any other algebraic equation: the left side of the equation must always equal the right side of the equation. The double-entry concept maintains the equality of the equation.

A more detailed examination of the components of the equation follows.

### Assets

Items of value that the business owns are assets, including tangible goods and future benefits. Examples of assets include cash; accounts receivable; inventories (such as materials, land, work in progress, finished units, office furniture and equipment, construction equipment and vehicles, and prepaid expenses).

Some assets are intangible; they represent future benefits and/or rights. For example, accounts receivable represent the right to collect cash some time in the future; prepaid expenses represent the right to receive a service in the future. Most of the assets for a typical home building and a land development company are inventories: houses under construction, land to be developed, or land in the process of being developed. However, remodelers do not have much in the way of inventory (except for construction materials) because typically they do not own the properties they work on.

### Equities

Claims to the assets of a business by creditors, lenders, owners, and investors are equities. Generally, the claims of creditors and lenders are referred to as liabilities. They include accounts payable, notes payable, and construction loans payable. The claims of owners are referred to as owners' equity. Owners' equity consists of two pieces: the owners' investment and the accumulation of net income or losses commonly known as retained earnings. The owners bear the risk of operating the business. Thus, they increase their portion of the equity if the business makes a profit, or they reduce their equity if the business loses money.

Go back to the accounting equation. Through the operation of the business, the assets of the new company now equal $700,000, and the equation now looks like the following one:

Assets = Equities

$700,000 = $700,000

If you break down the equities into third parties' equity and owners' equity, the equity side of the equation looks as follows:

$$\text{Equities} = \text{Liabilities} + \text{Owners' equity}$$
$$\$700{,}000 = \$500{,}000 + \$200{,}000$$

Putting both parts together, the equation looks is as follows:

$$\text{Assets} = \text{Liabilities} + \text{Owners' equity}$$
$$\$700{,}000 = \$500{,}000 + \$200{,}000$$

Remember that owners' equity represents not only the initial investment, but also the accumulated profit and loss (retained earnings) from the start of operations. As such, every time the company earns revenue, the owners' equity increases, and every time the company incurs an expense or cost, the owners' equity decreases. Any cash withdrawals, dividends, or distributions to the owners also decrease the owners' equity.

Chapter 7 discusses the elements of this equation in greater detail.

## Debits and Credits

The terms *debit* and *credit* become confusing to non-accountants because of the way they are used by bankers and retailers. When you return merchandise and the store is not willing to give you cash back, it issues a credit; or when your bank charges you a fee, it debits your account. Both retailers and bankers are communicating to you how the transaction affects their accounting records. When bankers or retailers issue a credit to you, they create a liability or an obligation to provide you with cash or services in the future. Because their liability increases and liabilities carry a credit balance, they credit your account. Simultaneously, you receive the promise or the right to future value, which for you is an asset. Therefore, you have a debit because your assets have increased. When bankers or retailers issue a debit to your account, they have either charged you a fee, or they have given you either cash or merchandise. In effect, they released an obligation to you or created an obligation from you. If they released an obligation or a liability, they debit your account to decrease the liability because liabilities have credit balances. If they created an obligation from you, they also created an asset for them. Therefore, they also debit their books to increase their assets.

The terms *debit* and *credit* are meaningless unless they are used in conjunction with the general accounting classifications of assets, liabilities, and owners' equity. In the equations used throughout this book the symbols *Dr* and *Cr* represent the terms *debit* and *credit*: By convention, assets are represented by debit balances, and liabilities and owners' equity by credit balances as follows:

$$\text{Assets} = \text{Liabilities} + \text{Owners' equity}$$
$$\text{Dr} \quad = \quad \text{Cr} \quad + \quad \text{Cr}$$

To take another approach to understanding debits and credits, return to the basic mathematical principles of adding like signs and subtracting signs that are different. For example, under mathematical principles, you always add two or more positive numbers as well as two or more negative numbers; in both instances you are dealing with like signs. When you have a negative number and a positive number, subtract one number from the other, and the sign of the higher value prevails. The same is true when working with debits and credits.

Examining the accounting equation, if you add the two credits on the right side of the equation, you validate the equality of the equation as follows:

$$\$700,000 = \$500,000 + \$200,000$$
$$\$700,000 = \$700,000$$

When the data entry clerk records financial transactions, the first step is to determine the traditional balance of the accounts affected by the transaction, and the second is to determine if the transaction increases or decreases the account.

For example, for the initial entry made at the start of the company an owner set up a business account at a bank in the amount of $200,000. The cash deposit increased the assets of the company. Cash is recognized as an asset represented by debit balances. Thus, to increase the cash account from $0 to $200,000, the company debited the account. The complementary side of this transaction is the source of the cash: it came from the owner, which means the owner's equity increased from $0 to $200,000. Because the owner's equity is represented by a credit balance, the company increased the owner's equity by crediting the owner's equity account. The transaction will look as follows:

Debit cash (asset) for $200,000

Credit capital contribution (owner's equity) for $200,000

Using the accounting equation format results in the following transaction:

Assets = Liabilities + Owner's equity
$$\$200,000 = \quad 0 \quad + \$200,000$$

Thus, builders, remodelers, and developers can presume the following generalities.

- To increase assets that are generally represented by debit balances (Dr), debit the assets: Dr + Dr.
- To increase liabilities that generally are represented by credit balances (Cr), credit the liability: Cr + Cr.
- To increase owners' equity that generally is represented by credit balances (Cr), credit the owners' equity: Cr + Cr.
- To decrease assets that generally are represented by debit balances (Dr), credit the assets: Dr − Cr.
- To decrease liabilities that generally are represented by credit balances (Cr), debit the liability: Cr − Dr.
- To decrease owners' equity that generally is represented by credit balances (Cr), debit the owners' equity: Cr − Dr.

Although today's software systems may provide guidance on how to record transactions, users must understand the logic behind each transaction. Understanding this logic helps users pinpoint errors critical to accurate and reliable reports.

Examine examples of how to record typical financial transactions. Figures 2.4–2.7 provide examples of how to record typical financial transactions. They also illustrate the effect the transactions have on the accounting equation by

**Figure 2.4** Purchase office equipment

A company buys two computers and a printer for the office. It pays $1,000 in cash, and the owner signs a note to pay off the balance of $3,000 in monthly installments of $250 per month, plus interest.

Analysis of the transaction reveals the following:

1. The company acquires assets (office equipment) valued at $4,000 and, thus, increases the company's total assets.
2. The company uses $1,000 cash, also an asset, to purchase the equipment, thus reducing its cash assets by $1,000.
3. The owner signs a note promising to pay a creditor the balance of $3,000, in monthly installments of $250, plus interest, which increases the company's liabilities.

The accounting equation for this transaction follows:

      Assets  =  Liabilities + Owners' equity

1. Dr $4,000
2. Cr ($1,000)
3.              Cr $3,000
      —————————————————————————
      $3,000 =    $3,000

The company pays the first $250 installment as follows:

1. Cash, an asset, is reduced by $250.
2. Notes payable, a liability, is reduced by $250.

      Assets  =  Liabilities + Owners' equity

1. Cr ($250)
2.              Dr ($250)
      —————————————————————————
      $250  =    $250

showing how each entry affects the equation and how the equality and integrity of the system is maintained.

Stores and financial institutions contribute to our confusion about debits and credits. Banks and stores use debits and credits to reflect what happens to their accounting records when a client or customer makes a transaction rather than to show how the transaction affects the client's records. For example, when someone opens a checking account at a bank and makes a deposit, a claim is created on the assets of the bank. In other words, the client has the right to withdraw the funds at any time. The bank is merely holding the funds owned by the client. The bank's accounting records show the claim as a liability or credit because it represents an obligation on the part of the bank to return the cash to the account holder upon

**Figure 2.5**  Purchase a finished lot

A company deposits $10,999 for a lot costing $70,000. The company

2. Commits a deposit of $10,000 for future rights to buy a lot, thus increasing its assets
3. Pays $10,000 in cash for the right to purchase the lot, thus decreasing an asset

      Assets  =  Liabilities  +  Owners' equity
1. Dr  $10,000
2. Cr ($10,000)
         0   =   0

The company closes on the lot and takes ownership. The company

1. Acquires an asset—the lot—thus increasing its assets by $70,000
2. Applies the $10,000 deposit (an asset) to the total cost of the lot, thus decreasing the company's assets
3. Uses a $60,000 loan, a liability, to finance the balance on the lot

      Assets  =  Liabilities  +  Owners' equity
1. Dr  $70,000
2. Cr ($10,000)
3.             Cr  $60,000
    $60,000 =    $60,000

**Figure 2.6**  Purchase a parcel of raw land

A developer purchases a small parcel of undeveloped land for $750,000, with the following terms: $100,000 in cash and a loan of $650,000 payable over five years at 10% interest in quarterly installments. When the contract closes, it affects the following accounts:

1. Cash, an asset, decreases $100,000.
2. Land, an asset, increases $750,000.
3. Notes payable, a liability, increases $650,000.

Placing the transaction in the accounting equation helps to verify that the transaction balances as follows:

      Assets  =  Liabilities  +  Owners' equity
1. Cr ($100,000)
2. Dr  $750,000
2.             Cr $650,000
    $650,000 =    $650,000

**Figure 2.7** Sale of a house

A builder sells a house for $250,000 and pays a sales commission of 6%. The seller pays closing costs totaling $2.250 for the buyer. The cost of the house includes land, $44,000, and construction, $150,900. Loans on the property total $173,000. Analyzing the transaction produces the following results:

1. The company realizes revenues, so owners' equity increases by $250,000.
2. The builder incurs expenses associated with the sale, and owner's equity declines by $15,000 (sales commission) plus $2,250 (closing costs).
3. The builder repays the loan and reduces the loans payable account, a liability, by $173,000.
4. The builder receives cash, so cash assets increase by $59,700.
5. To account for the costs associated with the sale, owner's equity declines by $194,900 (land, $44,000; construction costs, $150,900).
6. The sale reduces inventories. Land, an asset, declines by $44,000, and construction costs (work in process), an asset, declines by $150,900.

|  | Assets | = | Liabilities | + | Owners' equity |
|---|---|---|---|---|---|
| 1. |  |  |  |  | Cr $250,000 |
| 2. |  |  |  |  | Dr $15,000 + $2300 |
| 3. |  |  | Dr $173,000 |  |  |
| 4. | Dr $59,700 |  |  |  |  |
| 5. |  |  |  |  | Dr $44,000 + $150,900 |
| 6. | Cr $44,000 + $150,900 |  |  |  |  |

$$($135,200) = ($173,000) + $37,800$$
$$($135,200) = ($135,200)$$

demand. With every new deposit, the claim increases and the bank credits the client's account to show the increase in the bank's liability. Conversely, when the client takes money out of the account, the claim is satisfied, the liability is decreased, and thus the account is debited.

Translating such a transaction to a company's accounting records can be confusing. The transaction will be the reverse of the one recorded in the bank's accounting system. When a company makes a deposit to a bank account, the cash balance on the account increases and creates a debit to the cash account in the company's records. Conversely, a withdrawal decreases the asset and requires a credit to the cash account.

## Net Income or Loss

After a sale, the company deducts all costs and expenses and is left with the net income or net loss. To compute net income, subtract from sales the cost of sales (lot and direct construction cost on houses sold), operating expenses, and all expenses necessary to run the business. As stated earlier, owners' equity accumulates the results of operations from prior years. Revenues or sales increase the owners' equity, and conversely, cost of sales and operating expenses decrease the owners' equity as follows:

Net income (loss) = Revenues − Cost of sales = Operating expenses

Revenues and expenses fit in the accounting equation as follows:

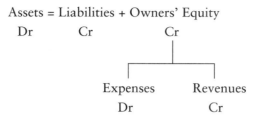

Cost of sales and operating expenses are both considered expenses under the broad definition of expense because they both reduce owners' equity.

### Revenues

This term represents the money earned from providing goods and services to third parties. All profit-oriented organizations are in business to generate revenue. For the home builder or remodeler, sales of houses or remodeling jobs are the most important sources of revenue. For developers, the main source of revenue is the sale of developed tracts of land or finished lots. Revenues are represented by credit balances because they increase owners' equity.

### Cost of Sales

The term *cost* is distinct from the term *expense*. Cost is associated with the creation of value, and therefore, it is considered an asset, an item of value the business owns prior to a sale. Costs that create value include homes under construction and the associated cost of materials and labor. As construction progresses, the costs of materials and labor add value to the house and increase the value of the asset. In this case, the asset is work-in-progress inventory.

Why, then, does cost of sales reduce owners' equity? When a house is sold, the company no longer has the right to the asset, even though the sale generates revenues. The cost of the house then becomes an expense normally known as cost of sales. That cost reduces the amount of revenue received on the transaction and, thus, decreases the owners' equity.

### Direct and Indirect Construction Cost

Builders, remodelers, and developers deal with two types of construction costs: direct and indirect.

**Direct construction costs.** These costs are easily identified because owners and managers can trace them to a specific unit of production: the cost of lumber, bricks, paint, and kitchen appliances (for builders and remodelers); materials such as asphalt for roads (for developers); and the cost of labor hours for the trades such as excavators, framers, roofers, and masons. These costs create value. Therefore, they increase the value of the work-in-process inventories.

Indirect construction costs. These costs relate to the construction process itself rather than to a particular unit of production. Indirect construction costs include salaries of field supervisors, field offices, field vehicles, temporary utilities, storage facilities, mobile/cell phones, and any other expense necessary to carry out the construction process. These costs also create value. Therefore, builders, remodelers, and developers should add them to the work-in-progress costs because they are part of the cost of building a house, completing a remodeling job, or developing a tract of land.

Builders, remodelers, and developers commonly refer to indirect construction costs as *overhead* and *soft costs*. These terms generally include indirect construction costs plus some or all other operating expenses. Therefore, whenever someone uses the term *overhead* or *soft cost*, be sure you understand the types of costs and expenses to which it refers. Future chapters will expand on the concept of how to account for and manage these costs, and they will explain how to allocate them to cost of sales and work-in-progress inventory.

## Operating Expenses

Builders, remodelers, and developers necessarily incur operating expenditures in operating their businesses. Generally, these expenses are associated with a given time period—a month, a quarter, or a year—rather than with a unit of production. Therefore, owners and managers commonly refer to them as period costs. In accounting, their bookkeepers subtract operating expenses for a given period from revenues received during the same time period.

To manage different types of expenses, owners and managers should further classify expenses into functions or departments, such as financing, sales and marketing, and general and administrative expenses. These expenses relate to the passage of time not to units of production.

### Financing Expenses

Financing expenses represent the cost of borrowing money from financial institutions or other third party sources. Owners and managers often can trace financing expenses directly to a specific house or project. In fact, under certain circumstances, tax legislation requires that builders, remodelers, and developers relate financing expenses directly to units of production. Therefore, they should charge these expenses to the asset account as a direct construction cost instead of to the expense account. For management purposes, builders, remodelers, and developers should also set up interest accounts as operating expenses. To ensure that they are following the law, builders, remodelers, and developers should consult annually with an accountant or tax consultant who is familiar with the law.

### Sales and Marketing Expenses

Sales and marketing expenses are associated with a given time period and are charged against the revenues received during the same period. In certain instances, builders must capitalize certain marketing expenses. Refer to Chapter 15 for capitalization rules on sales and marketing expenses.

When a marketing expense will benefit more than one accounting period such as development of the marketing campaign for a new community that will take three years to build, the cost of developing the campaign might need to be spread over the three years. The process will be to capitalize the total amount or record the amount in an asset account that clearly identifies the nature of the expenditure and expense proportionally to each accounting period.

Many builders add the commissions paid on the sale of the house to the cost of sales. However, even though commissions are associated with each house sold, builders should accumulate commissions in the expense category. This practice allows the owner or manager to evaluate the true cost of marketing and selling all houses and to determine if this function is being carried out effectively and efficiently.

### General and Administrative Expenses

Expenses other than construction operations, financing, and sales and marketing that are necessary to operate a business are general and administrative expenses. They include office supplies, telephone service, administrative salaries, office rent, books and subscriptions, insurance, and so on. They are associated with a specific time period rather than to a particular home, lot, or job and are charged against revenues received during the same time.

Figure 2.8 shows how costs flow through various accounts from the time the cost is incurred to the closing of the sale.

**Figure 2.8**  Flow of costs through the system

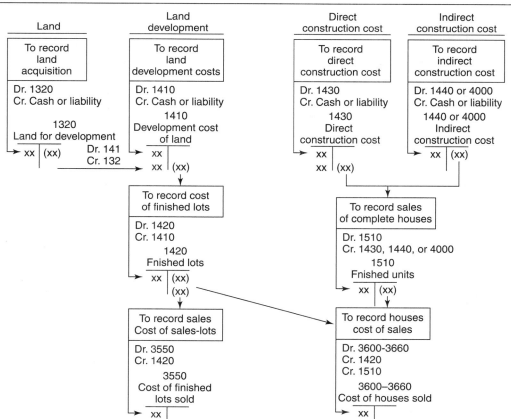

To summarize the concepts presented in this section, *assets* represent items of value owned by the business; *equities* identify who claims the assets, either creditors or owners. *Revenues* and *expenses* measure profits or losses, and in turn, profits and losses impact the owners' share of the assets.

## Financial Statements

The two most commonly used financial statements produced by the accounting system are the income statement (also known as the profit-and-loss statement) and the balance sheet. These financial statements

- summarize the result of the financial transactions occurring during a particular time period
- identify whether a profit or loss was generated
- examine how that profit or loss affects the position of the lenders and owners of the company

### Income Statement

The income statement summarizes the results of a company's operations for a given time period, such as a month, a quarter, or a year. The income statement covers all revenue sources as well as the costs associated with them and the operating

**Figure 2.9** ABC Homes income statement

| ABC Homes Income Statement Year ended December 31, 20__ | |
|---|---|
| Sales | $ 10,691,000 |
| Cost of sales | 9,621,900 |
| Gross profit | $ 1,069,100 |
| | |
| Expenses: | |
| Advertising | 106,900 |
| Auto expenses | 24,900 |
| Contributions | 4,000 |
| Depreciation | 16,400 |
| Insurance | 25,500 |
| Maintenance and repairs | 10,850 |
| Rent | 43,200 |
| Office supplies | 15,700 |
| Salaries | 390,730 |
| Small tools | 9,780 |
| Telephone | 15,660 |
| Miscellaneous | 31,294 |
| Total expenses | 694,914 |
| Net income | $ 374,186 |

**Figure 2.10** ABC Homes income statement by function

**ABC Homes**
**Income Statement**
**Year ended December 31, 20__**

| | | |
|---|---|---|
| Sales | | $10,691,000 |
| Cost of sales | | |
| Land (lots) | $1,924,380 | |
| Direct construction costs | 6,414,600 | |
| Total cost of sales | | 8,338,980 |
| Gross profit | | $ 2,352,020 |
| | | |
| Operating expenses | | |
| Indirect construction costs | $ 406,258 | |
| Financing expenses | 374,184 | |
| Sales and marketing expenses | 694,916 | |
| General and administrative | 502,476 | |
| Total operating expenses | | 1,977,834 |
| | | |
| Net income | | $ 374,186 |

expenses for the reporting period. The result is the net income or net loss produced by the company during the reporting period as the following equation indicates:

Net income = Revenues − Cost of sales − Operating expense

The income statement is dynamic; its format determines how much information a builder, remodeler, or developer can obtain from it. The statement comprises three main sections: the revenues, the cost of sales, and the operating expenses. Group operating expenses by function or department: construction, financing, sales and marketing, general and administrative (with a subtotal after each category), so you can easily see the resources each function or department consumed. This approach assists in the quick measuring of each function or department's efficiency.

Operating expenses sometimes are listed alphabetically. This format hampers the analysis of how well each function or department performed during the period.

Two examples of income statements follow. Figure 2.9 provides little information about the company's operations, other than sales totaling $10,691,000 and a small profit. The income statement reveals how much the company spent on each line item, but not how each function or department performed. In contrast, fig. 2.10 shows the following details:

- which functions or departments spent the dollars
- lot costs
- cost of building the houses
- cost of running each function or department

*Balance Sheet*

In contrast to the income statement, the balance sheet is a snapshot of the financial position of a business as of the date shown on the statement. It shows the company's assets and who has claims to them: creditors, lenders, or owners. The following equation represents the balance sheet:

Assets = Liabilities + Owners' equity

The balance sheet classifies assets and liabilities as either current or long-term and other items. Classifying the numbers this way enables calculation of a key financial ratio to evaluate the company's solvency. *Current assets* are assets that could be converted into cash within a 12-month period, and *current liabilities* are obligations to be paid within a 12-month period (fig. 2.11).

As you can see, the amount in total assets equals the amount in total liabilities and owners' equity; thus these amounts verify the equality of the equation.

Chapter 7 includes a detailed discussion of the income statement and balance sheet. The financial statements classify the numbers to help builders, remodelers, and developers measure performance and make decisions about their businesses. Financial statements allow owners and managers to compare current results with prior years and with industry performance. By analyzing trends and financial ra-

**Figure 2.11** ABC Homes balance sheet

| | |
|---|---|
| **ABC Homes** | |
| **Balance Sheet** | |
| **December 31, 20__** | |
| | |
| **Assets** | |
| Current assets | |
| Cash | $    985,000 |
| Inventories—land | 5,200,000 |
| Inventories—work in process | 6,500,000 |
| Total current assets | $12,685,000 |
| Other assets | 1,450,000 |
| Total assets | $14,135,000 |
| | |
| **Liabilities and Owners' Equity** | |
| Liabilities | |
| Current liabilities | $ 7,200,000 |
| Long-term liabilities | 4,300,000 |
| Total liabilities | $11,500,000 |
| Owners' equity | 2,635,000 |
| Total liabilities and owners' equity | $14,135,000 |

tios as well, owners and managers gain additional insights about the company's strengths and weaknesses, and they can concentrate their efforts on improving poorly performing functions and departments.

Chapter 8 discusses in detail how to use financial analysis techniques to improve business operations and profitability.

# Users of Financial Information

Lenders, investors, taxing authorities, owners, and managers use company financial information for various reasons. The following sections describe the specific needs of each group.

### Owners and Managers

Owners and managers of home building, remodeling, and development companies are the primary users of the financial information the accounting system generates. Therefore, financial reports should allow ongoing monitoring of the return on investment and the company's overall health

The owners who set the general goals and direction for their companies find value in ratio and trend analysis. Managers who monitor the day-to-day operations of the company need more detailed reports. They use financial statements and management reports to measure performance and evaluate company profitability with timely comparisons of actual results with budgets or plans. Among other factors, the scope of a manager's responsibility determines the reports and level of detail he or she requires. The broader the scope, the more information the manager has to sort through; thus, standard reports need to be summarized. As employees' scopes narrow, they need even more detailed reports.

### Lenders

Lenders need to determine whether builders, remodelers, and developers can repay the loans they request. To measure liquidity, the owners' investment, and profitability, lenders almost exclusively focus on traditional financial statements: the balance sheet and the income statement. Sometimes, lenders also require certification or an opinion about the financial statements from an independent CPA.

### Investors

Investors also use the traditional financial statements to forecast the potential profitability of an investment. Analyzing the income statement and the balance sheet can disclose profitability, leverage factor, liquidity, holding power, and risk factor. In addition, comparing financial information for a number of consecutive years shows trends and provides potential investors with additional insight about company profitability.

The term *leverage factor* refers to how much third-party financing the owner is using to run the company compared with owner's capital. The more third-party financing used, the higher the leverage factor and as a consequence the higher the risk. *Holding power* refers to how long the company would be able to stay in business during a down turn or when sales are not occurring at the anticipated velocity.

## Reporting Requirements

Requirements for reporting vary significantly from company to company depending upon the sales volume and number of employees. Large, midsize, and small companies should prepare financial statements (balance sheet and income statement) at least monthly. Beyond these reports, the more employees a company has, the more reports it will require to support owners' and managers' decision-making as these employees become further removed from the front line. For example, line managers (who direct the actual construction, remodeling, or development process) need reports with cost codes that measure the details of the different construction phases and how they compare to predetermined or estimated costs. However, companies should resist the temptation of current technology's ability to produce an overabundance of highly detailed reports. Producing and reviewing unnecessary reports wastes time and distracts users from the main issues. To determine the value of a report, ask if it will guide action. If not, the report probably is unnecessary.

## Audit Trail

The IRS requires adequate recordkeeping with a strong audit trail to verify the accuracy and legitimacy of the company's tax returns. Reviews and audits performed by CPA firms require an audit trail that traces financial transactions to their original documents (an original invoice, for example).

As the owner or president of the company delegates authority to managers and employees, the owner or president's control over financial transactions diminishes. Therefore, an annual audit is a wise investment for medium to large building companies with layers of management. An annual audit verifies that performance of financial transactions follows established processes and procedures and can detect fraud. It also verifies that the company keeps its records according to GAAP.

Reducing the risk of fraud requires an internal system of checks and balances. A critical piece of this system of checks and balances segregates such functions as recordkeeping, custodianship of assets, authorization for use of assets, and operations. For example, whenever possible, purchasing, accounting, check writing, and check signing should be carried out by different employees. In a small-volume firm in which one individual might be responsible for more than one of these functions, the owner should maintain control of, at least, the check-signing function.

# CHAPTER 3

# Accounting Methods and Terms

uilders, remodelers, and developers can use various methods to maintain accounting records and keep track of revenues, costs, and expenses. The chosen method to process data does not alter system effectiveness although procedures and output may vary slightly. This chapter provides an overview of some of the methods and discusses accounting practices and terminology common to the home building industry.

One purpose of accounting is to measure net income or profits for a given period. When calculating profits, a primary concern is determining which costs and expenses relate to revenues earned. A builder, remodeler, or developer can choose among different methods to record revenues, costs, and expenses as follows:

- Cash or accrual relates to the timing for entering transactions in the system.
- Completed contract or percentage of completion relates to the procedure for recognizing revenues.
- Direct costing or absorption costing relates to the procedure for allocating construction costs to units of production (houses, remodeling jobs, or lots).

## Cash or Accrual

Builders, remodelers, and developers may use either the cash method or the accrual method to record financial transactions.

The *accrual* method provides more timely and accurate information because the bookkeeper enters the transactions as they occur, independent of when cash changes hands. One drawback of this method is the need to track the cash exchange when it occurs. In contrast, the *cash* method is less complicated and, therefore, easier to use. It can be effective for small-volume companies with an owner who is a hands-on manager. However, one disadvantage of the cash accounting method is timing. Because transactions are not recorded until the cash exchange occurs, a significant amount of time can elapse before a transaction is recorded and shows up in the company's reports.

### Cash

Regardless of when a company earns revenues or incurs expenses, a cash accounting system reports revenues, costs, and expenses in the accounting period in which cash is received or disbursed. The bookkeeper records only the cash transactions (that is, the cash deposits made on a given day) and the checks written on the same day. Financial statements and management reports do not reflect current financial conditions because of (1) the time lag between recognition of revenues and actual receipt of cash and (2) the delay between commitment to cost or expenses and the actual cash disbursement. However, a cash system that records only cash exchanges is the easiest way to keep financial records.

### Accrual

Regardless of when a cash transaction takes place, an accrual accounting system records revenues and expenses when they are earned and incurred. For this reason, reports done under the accrual system are more current.

For example, the invoice for materials purchased on January 27, after the supplier's billing closes for the month, would not appear in the supplier's statement to the customer until February. Payment would not be due until March 31, two months after the customer incurred the cost. Under the cash method, the invoice would be entered in the accounting system when the check is written—as late as March 31. Under the accrual method, the bookkeeper records the purchase after he or she receives the invoice with the verification from the field that the materials have been received as ordered and in good condition.

A common misconception of the accrual system is that it hinders the control of cash because revenues and expenses do not measure cash inflows and outflows recorded in the cash account. However, the accrual method helps builders, remodelers, and developers better manage cash flow. Remember that under the accrual method, cash received but not earned is a liability rather than income, whereas the cash system recognizes cash as income when it is received. Generally, a contract to sell a home or lot requires a deposit, but buyers sometimes cancel contracts before closing, and the deposits usually are returned. Under the cash system, though, the deposits probably already would have been counted as revenues. Therefore, returning a deposit would reduce revenues. Remodelers also usually collect deposits on signed contracts. But even if a home owner cancels a remodeling contract, the remodeler may have earned the amount of the deposit for work done prior to the cancellation.

Under the accrual system, the right to receive cash is entered as an asset in a receivable account, and the obligation to pay cash is entered as a liability in a payable account. Therefore, the accrual method shows the dollar amount the company is entitled to collect and also the dollar amount the company is obligated to pay. This arrangement makes managing cash flow easier.

Lenders and potential investors favor the use of the accrual system because it presents a more comprehensive picture of the company's financial condition. It clearly matches revenues and expenses more accurately than the cash system, and it presents a timelier picture of the company's financial condition.

# Completed Contract or Percentage of Completion

Builders sometimes work on projects extending over several fiscal or calendar years. For these projects, both the completed contract and the percentage of completion accounting methods are acceptable. However, the percentage of completion method can only be used for jobs that are sold or built under enforceable contracts and are in progress at the end of the accounting period for a particular month, quarter, or year.

The method selected will affect taxable income for the given year. Therefore, tax regulations might determine which method to use based on the average dollar volume of revenues for the prior three years and the nature of the construction activity. Current regulations exempt any home building activity from having to be recorded under the percentage of completion method regardless of the dollar volume of the company. But because tax regulations are subject to change from year to year, make sure you and your tax accountant comply with the current directives. The cost for speculative jobs must accrue in an inventory (asset) account, and you cannot recognize any revenues from such a job until the sale closes.

### Completed Contract

Home builders (especially production builders), remodelers, and developers typically use this completed contract method to recognize income and cost of sales. This method recognizes neither revenues nor cost of sales until work is completed and the sales contract has been fully executed or closed. In the interim, the bookkeeper records all costs related to the contract in an inventory account, and the cash received for the job (advance payments or contract deposits) goes into a liability account or deferred revenue account. When the buyer takes possession of the house, the bookkeeper transfers the costs to a cost-of-sales account and the contract deposits to a revenue account. For tax purposes, this method is more favorable to use because under current tax regulations, home builders can report sales using the completed contract method, regardless of their sales volume.

### Percentage of Completion

The percentage of completion method recognizes revenues and cost of sales as the job progresses. It can only be used for jobs being built under contract such as a custom home or a remodeling job. Commercial or light industrial construction projects are subject to IRS rules regarding sales volume. If a commercial or light industrial builder's average sales volume for the prior three years exceeds the limit set by the IRS, the builder must report revenues from all commercial or light construction activities using the percentage of completion method.

To determine the percentage of revenues earned on contracts at the end of each accounting period, calculate the percentage of completion for each job based on observation. Then, apply the percentage to (1) the total value of the contract to establish the revenues earned to date and (2) the total estimated costs, to determine the cost of sales to date. Thus, if a job extends over several years and construction is 40% complete at the end of an accounting period, you would recognize 40% of the contract price as revenue, and 40% of the total estimated cost of sales. At completion of the job, the total amount of revenues recognized during more than one accounting period must equal the total amount of the contract, and the total cost of sales must equal the total cost during the life of the project.

Under either method, total revenues and cost of sales on the job will be the same; the difference is in when you recognize the revenues and cost of sales. The percentage-of-completion method is more time consuming because it requires additional calculations and entries at the end of each month. Advocates of the percentage-of-completion method argue that it measures the performance of the company more accurately because it recognizes revenue throughout the construction period, and it matches revenue more closely with operating expenses. However, well-trained and experienced managers understand the dynamics of long-term contracts and do not need this approach to see the relationship between revenue and operating expenses. The tax consequences and additional accounting staff time that percentage of completion requires provide valid reasons to discourage the use of this method by home builders.

Another word of caution: calculating the percent of completion can be tricky for some jobs. The amount recognized as revenue is no more accurate than an estimate would be. Be careful with your calculations of percent completed; otherwise, the resulting reports can be misleading and falsely represent your company's financial status.

## Direct and Absorption Costing

*Costing* means allocating construction costs to units of production, such as finished lots, houses, or remodeling jobs. Direct costing and absorption costing are two methods of accumulating cost. Even though direct costing is an analytical tool in managerial accounting, the AICPA and the IRS recognize absorption costing as the accepted method for product costing.

### Direct Costing

Cost can be classified as either direct or indirect. *Direct construction costs* include the material and labor to build the homes; *indirect construction costs* are incurred in the construction process but do not become part of the homes. Examples of direct construction costs are all the materials used in building the home (lumber, bricks, drywall, and the like) and the labor to put up the materials (framers, drywallers, roofers, and so on). Examples of indirect construction costs include the salaries of the superintendents (they do not work on the houses; they supervise the construction) and the cost of the field office, trucks, telephones, and electronic devices (they are needed to run the jobsites, but they do not become part of the homes).

Under the direct costing method, only direct costs are included in the cost of sales for each home. Indirect costs are considered period costs, and they are charged against revenues in the period in which they are incurred. Even though direct costing does not comply with GAAP or the IRS rules, this method helps builders, remodelers, and developers analyze each cost and expense component. An accountant can readily convert direct costing to absorption costing.

### Absorption Costing

When using absorption costing, both direct and indirect costs become part of a home's cost. As a result, when builders, remodelers, or developers use this method, inventories show a greater dollar value, and the income statement shows a higher net income.

**Figure 3.1** Direct costing versus absorption costing

During the month of January, a builder constructs three houses at a direct cost of $160,000 each, including the land cost. The total indirect cost is $27,000, or $9,000 per unit. Two houses are sold for $230,000 each; one house remains in inventory. Operating expenses for the month amount to $70,000.

|  | Direct Costing | Absorption Costing |
|---|---|---|
| Inventory valuation |  |  |
|   Direct cost | $160,000 | $160,000 |
|   Indirect cost |  | 9,000 |
|   Total | $160,000 | $169,000 |
| Cost of sales |  |  |
|   Direct cost (2 houses) | $320,000 | $320,000 |
|   Indirect cost |  | 18,000 |
|   Total | $320,000 | $338,000 |
| Net income (January) |  |  |
|   Sales | $460,000 | $460,000 |
|   Cost of sales | 320,000 | 338,000 |
|   Gross profit | $140,000 | $122,000 |
|   Indirect cost | $ 27,000 |  |
|   Operating expenses | 70,000 | $  70,000 |
|   Net income | $ 43,000 | $  52,000 |
| House closed (February) |  |  |
|   Sales | $230,000 | $230,000 |
|   Cost of sales | 160,000 | 169,000 |
|   Gross profit | $ 70,000 | $ 61,000 |
| Total net income | $113,000 | $113,000 |

Figure 3.1 compares direct and absorption costing and the results for a builder closing three homes: the net income from the three homes is identical under both methods even though income is recognized at different points, according to the method used.

## Accounting Terminology

A number of accounting terms are often misused or misunderstood. This section identifies and explains the most commonly misunderstood terms and their significance in accounting.

### Revenues Versus Cash Receipts

Revenues and cash are not the same, not even when using the cash system of accounting. Cash receipts do not come only from revenue sources. Cash also comes from accounts receivable collected, proceeds from the sale of a fixed asset (i.e., furniture or equipment); refunds on returned merchandise; capital contributions from owners; and loans.

### Expenses Versus Cash Disbursements

At the same time, all cash disbursements are not necessarily expenses or costs. Cash disbursements may be for investments in land; equipment; securities; or payments on loans, dividends, or accounts payable. Furthermore, under either a cash or an accrual system, you still must recognize them and record some expenses that do not require a cash disbursement, such as depreciation.

### Profit Versus Cash Balance

Because all cash receipts are not considered revenues and all cash disbursements are not expenses, a company's cash balance cannot possibly equal profits. Profits and cash are separate measurements of distinct elements of a company's finances: (1) revenues and expenses for profits and (2) cash sources and disbursements for cash balance. Under no circumstances is one a measure of the other, but both are extremely important to track and manage to ensure the company's survival.

### Expenses Versus Cost

The terms *expense* and *cost* are not interchangeable: cost is associated with a manufacturing process and is considered a business asset until the manufactured product, such as a new house, is sold. Building companies accumulate costs in an inventory account representing the value of the homes under construction. However, expenses relate to day-to-day business operations. Accountants sometimes refer to expenses as period costs because they are charged off against revenues received during the same time period in which the expenses are incurred. Examples of such expenses include rent, insurance, telephone, advertising, interest, and commissions.

### Indirect Construction Cost Versus Overhead

Indirect construction costs, sometimes referred to as *soft costs*, are the costs associated with the building process. They cannot be traced directly to any particular unit of production, only to the construction process. Overhead could be the same as indirect construction costs, but sales expenses, financing expenses, and a portion of the general and administrative expenses typically also are part of overhead. Because overhead can include indirect costs and one or more types of expenses, clarify what is and is not included.

### Fixed Versus Variable Cost or Expense

Costs and expenses are either fixed or variable. Fixed costs and expenses remain constant within a volume range: in other words, they do not change with the number of homes built within a set volume range. The more units produced within the range, the lower the cost per unit; conversely, the lower the number of units, the higher the cost per unit. Operating at the higher end of a volume range would provide operational efficiencies.

Fixed costs and expenses (typically personnel costs, leases on space and equipment, and office costs) are generally controlled by the owner or top level managers. On a per unit basis, fixed costs and expenses change as the number of homes, jobs, or lots developed changes. They increase on a per-unit basis when volume drops and decrease on a per-unit basis when volume increases.

In contrast, variable costs and expenses increase or decrease proportionately with increases or decreases in the units of production. In other words, variable costs and expenses relate directly to the number of units built. The more units built, the higher the variable costs or expenses. For example, the cost for lumber increases in proportion to the number of houses built. By the same token, as production decreases, so do the variable costs and expenses. On a per-unit basis, variable costs remain constant.

Understanding the differences between fixed and variable costs and expenses and how each behaves helps builders, remodelers, and developers control processes. Generally, variable costs and expenses are controlled by lower level management; while owners and top level managers are responsible for controlling fixed costs and expenses. Efficiency and productivity are key concepts in controlling fixed costs and expenses because production levels significantly impact the per-unit cost.

# CHAPTER 4

# Chart of Accounts

Every accounting system requires a standardized format to accumulate and classify financial transactions as they occur. The format provides the sorting mechanism to process and convert the information into meaningful statements and reports. The NAHB Chart of Accounts is the preferred format for home building, remodeling, and development companies.

## Structure

A list of the accounts used to record and track financial transactions, the chart establishes a structure for the system and determines the level of detail for future reports. Each account focuses on a specific type of activity within five major categories (see Chapter 2):

- assets
- liabilities
- owners' equity
- revenues
- expenses

Because the chart of accounts is the foundation of the company's accounting system, the owner and company accountant should be involved in designing it to ensure that it meets criteria for both reporting and control.

As discussed in Chapter 2, the accounting system operates at two levels, the financial or general ledger and the managerial or subsidiary ledgers. At the financial level, the accounting system accumulates summary data and generates the income statement, the balance sheet, and other reports. Subsidiary ledgers accumulate data in a more detailed format for management analysis, reporting, and control. For example, the subsidiary ledgers generate job cost reports for each construction unit, job, or lot; status reports on construction loans; gross profit analysis on units sold; and other reports.

Use the following guidelines to design a chart of accounts:

■ Include the five general categories and group accounts under assets, liabilities, owners' equity, revenues, and expenses.

■ Allow data to be classified with sufficient detail to satisfy both fiscal requirements and management needs.

■ Group expenses by function or department to facilitate analysis: construction (indirect construction costs), financing, sales and marketing, and general and administrative.

A chart of accounts should remain consistent to ensure comparability with prior periods, plans, and budgets. At the same time, the chart of accounts must (1) allow future changes with minimum disruption to the system as a whole and (2) accommodate expansion to meet new financial and management requirements. Furthermore, the estimating, purchasing, and scheduling systems should be integrated with the job cost subsidiary system. Integrating these systems facilitates coordination and increases the efficiency of every department and at every level of operation.

## Numerical Coding System

A chart of accounts usually incorporates a numerical system to provide a convenient method of identifying each account, facilitate data entry and processing, and help structure reports. A well-designed numerical coding system assures standardization and allows flexibility. It also facilitates conversion from a manual accounting system to a computerized one.

The numerical coding must follow a logical sequence to help identify each account's general category and subcategory. A coding structure of four digits is satisfactory for small- to medium-volume builders, developers, and remodelers. Large-volume builders and developers may need as many as eight digits to accommodate additional detail and classifications. Expanding businesses may need to add one or two digits to the existing four-digit coding. However, a chart of accounts must be as simple as possible, and you should add digits to yours only when necessary.

The NAHB Charts of Accounts (Appendixes A through E) ensures uniformity and comparability of financial information within the building, remodeling, and land development industries.

The general accounting categories and their recommended numerical coding are as follows:

1000 Assets

2000 Liabilities and owners' equity

3000 Sales, revenues, and cost of sales

4000 Indirect construction cost (or construction expenses)

5000 Financing expenses

6000 Sales and marketing expenses

7000 Rental operations expenses

8000 General and administrative expenses

9000 Other income and expenses

The second digit in the numerical coding system generally identifies a subclassification within a general classification. An example follows:

**1000–1990 Assets**

1000 Cash

1100 Short-term investments

1200 Receivables

1300 Inventories

The third digit provides a further breakdown of each subclassification as follows:

**1000–1090 Cash**

1010 Petty cash

1020 Cash on deposit, general

1030 Cash on deposit, payroll

1040 Cash on deposit, savings, and money market

The fourth digit can provide further breakdown as follows:

**1020 Cash on deposit, general**

1021 Cash—First National Bank

1022 Cash—Second National Bank

1023 Cash—Great Northern Bank

1024 Cash—First Savings and Loan

## Customizing the Chart of Accounts

Appendix A provides an outline of the chart of accounts discussed in this chapter. It has been expanded to include special accounts used by remodelers, developers, and multiple-project and commercial builders. Appendix B provides descriptions of each account, including the type of data that accumulates in the account, and it explains the specific requirements for using the account. Appendix B also notes which accounts are exclusively for recording financial data from remodeling, development, and multple-project and commercial building activities. Appendix C outlines basic accounts for small-volume builders, remodelers, and developers. Most small-volume builders, remodelers, and developers use the major account classifications in this chart. However, some builders, remodelers, and developers might not use all of the accounts presented in this chart; others may need to add accounts. In other words, they customize the chart of accounts presented here to reflect the structure of their companies and the ways they do business.

# CHAPTER 5

# Bookkeeping Procedures

As discussed earlier, an accounting system consists of two tracks that operate simultaneously. The general accounting system generates the financial statements, and the managerial or subsidiary accounting system generates detailed management reports. Both contain the same financial information, but the subsidiary system breaks down the data into greater detail than the general ledger.

The land and construction costs flow through the accounting system in a similar manner whether the construction is speculative or custom. The system accumulates costs, house-by-house, in the job cost subsidiary with separate categories or job cost accounts for each type of cost incurred. At closing or contract completion, the accountant transfers the costs to the cost of sales accounts. An additional entry at closing records revenues earned in the transaction.

The accounting system described in this book is commonly referred to as a double-entry system. In double-entry bookkeeping, each financial transaction affects at least two accounts within the five major accounting categories: assets, liabilities, owners' equity, revenues, and expenses. Figure 5.1 provides an example of double-entry bookkeeping under the accrual method of accounting.

The total amount of the accounts in a subsidiary ledger must equal the balance shown on the general ledger account. To maintain this balance, every time a bookkeeper enters transactions in a general ledger account that is supported by a subsidiary, the bookkeeper must also enter the same amount in a subsidiary account.

With a computer, accounting software programs handle both entries simultaneously. However, any software program is only as good as its user, and bookkeepers must ensure that they are following proper procedures to be sure the program works as designed. Without a computer, bookkeepers must record transactions manually.

Some software programs have safeguards to ensure that the person entering the data cannot exit the transaction screen until he or she has entered the required details to take the transaction to the subsidiary ledger. However, many software systems do allow entries in general ledger accounts supported by subsidiaries without requiring an entry in the subsidiary. Thus, businesses need processes in place to ensure that transactions are recorded in both the general ledger and the

**Figure 5.1** Recording a construction invoice with double-entry bookkeeping

When XYZ Excavating submits an invoice for $2,520 for work completed and accepted on unit 782, the bookkeeper records the entries for the invoice in the general accounting and subsidiary systems with the following results:

1. The house under construction, an asset, increased in value by $2,530.
2. The company incurred an obligation, a liability, to pay the trade contractor for his or her services, also $2,530.
   - This transaction affects accounts in the general ledger system as well as the subsidiary systems as follows:
1. General ledger system

   Dr. Direct construction cost (Work in progress inventory)—an asset for $2,520

   Cr. Accounts payable—a liability for $2,520
2. Job cost subsidiary system

   Dr. Unit 782 under the job cost code, excavation, shows the $2,520 increase in cost.
3. Accounts payable subsidiary

   Cr. The account for XYZ Excavating shows that the company owes the trade contractor $2,520.
   - When XYZ Excavating is paid the following accounts are affected:
1. Cash, an asset, is reduced.
2. Accounts payable, a liability, decreases.
   - The bookkeeper recorded the transaction as follows:
1. General ledger system

   Dr. Accounts payable—a liability for $2,520

   Cr. Cash—an asset for $2,520
2. Accounts payable subsidiary

   Dr. The account for XYZ Excavating shows that the trade contractor has been paid $2,520.

subsidiaries when required. In addition, they need to reconcile general and subsidiary ledger accounts monthly.

## Information Flow

Financial information flows through the accounting system as follows:

- from the general and special journals, such as cash, sales, payroll
- to the general ledger
- to reports such as income statement, balance sheet, and cash flow

Accounting software systems make this flow transparent while the transactions happen behind the scene.

## Journals

Bookkeepers enter their companies' financial transactions in chronological sequence in *journals* or books of original entry. (In contrast, ledgers summarize financial transactions.) A bookkeeper can enter all financial transactions into the system through the general journal. However, to facilitate bookkeeping, the bookkeeper uses special journals to record payroll, sales, purchases, cash receipts, and cash disbursements. He or she enters each transaction in the type of journal relevant to the transaction.

Today, in a process called *posting*, computer systems automatically copy the transaction to both general ledger accounts and subsidiary ledgers (if applicable) as the bookkeeper enters the transaction in the journal. If a transaction affects the accounts payable account, some computer programs would post it to the general ledger and also to the subsidiary ledger to the specific vendor's account. Others require that the bookkeeper trigger the posting. In a manual system, the bookkeeper has to post the transactions by hand to the relevant accounts in the general ledger and to the subsidiary ledgers (if applicable).

Bookkeepers accumulate transactions that relate to a particular account in a ledger. The accounts in the NAHB Chart of Accounts appear in the general ledger. A subsidiary ledger accumulates transactions that relate to a particular account. It breaks down the accounts in a general ledger account such as accounts payable and direct construction cost. For accounts payable, the subsidiary ledger separates the transactions by vendor. For direct construction cost, the subsidiary ledger separates the transactions by homes.

### General Journal

A bookkeeper enters transactions as dollar amounts into a two-column record—one for debits, the other for credits—in chronological order. Each entry includes the date of the transaction, accounts affected by the transaction, and a short description. The bookkeeper records the debits in the left column and credits in the right one. After the bookkeeper records debits and credits, he or she adds a brief explanation for each item.

If the bookkeeper uses special journals, he or she uses the general journal only to record special transactions, adjustments, and end-of-month entries that generally require no cash inflows or cash disbursements. In many accounting software programs, the general journal looks similar to one in a paper system.

## Special Journals

Special journals facilitate entering financial transactions sequentially. In contrast to the general journal, special journals may have more than two columns. A multicolumn format designates separate columns for frequently used accounts. The type of special journal and the account determines whether the columns represent debits or credits. For example, the cash column in the cash receipts journal is a debit column, and the cash column in the cash disbursement journal is a credit column.

The appearance of the special journals varies by software system. Typically, specially designed screens accept each type of entry. In some systems, the entry screens look like the documents that are the source of the transaction such as checks, invoices, or deposit slips. The actual accounting entry is invisible to the user.

Unlike the general journal, entries in special journals do not require explanations because the name of the special journal or screen identifies the nature of the transactions. Payroll, sales, purchases, cash receipts, and cash disbursements are among the transactions recorded in special journals or on special screens.

# Ledgers

Special journals save the bookkeeper considerable time and reduce the likelihood of bookkeeping errors because bookkeepers only have to post the month-end totals of each column.

Ledgers summarize financial transactions by account. The bookkeeper first enters all financial information in chronological order in a journal. Then the bookkeeper transfers the financial information from the journal into the designated accounts in the general ledger and the applicable subsidiary ledgers. Figure 5.2 compares the general and subsidiary ledgers.

### General Ledger

The accounts listed in the chart of accounts mirror the accounts in the general ledger. It provides data for traditional financial statements and some management reports. Information in the general ledger usually is not detailed enough to help builders, remodelers, and developers make daily business decisions. However, they will find it useful in analyzing trends and overall profitability, establishing goals, and preparing plans for future performance.

### Subsidiary Ledgers

The bookkeeper keeps the details of general ledger accounts in the subsidiary ledgers. The total of all accounts in subsidiary ledgers must equal the balance of the general ledger account. The most commonly used subsidiary ledgers include the following:

- accounts receivable
- accounts payable
- job cost (a subsidiary for account 1430, direct construction cost)

**Accounts receivable subsidiary.** Transactions recorded in this ledger represent money due to the company for jobs in progress. This ledger

- maintains the record of each person or company that owes money to a builder, remodeler, or developer
- keeps tract of payments received
- reports outstanding balances as of a particular date.

**Accounts payable subsidiary.** This subsidiary maintains an account for each supplier, vendor, and trade contractor to whom the builder, remodeler, or developer owes money. The bookkeeper records invoices in the accounts payable gen-

**Figure 5.2** Levels of recording, general ledger and subsidiary ledgers

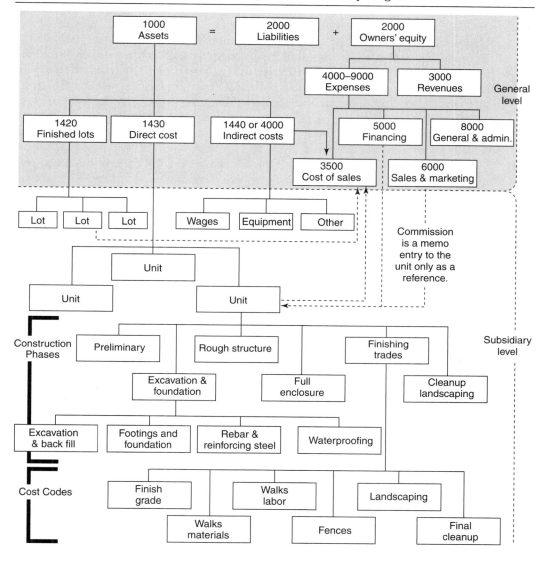

eral ledger account and in each creditor, supplier, or trade contractor account in the accounts payable subsidiary. When the bookkeeper records payments, he or she debits both the accounts payable general ledger account and the individual creditor account. The accounts payable subsidiary provides a historical record of all financial transactions with a particular supplier or trade contractor. The total of all accounts in the accounts payable subsidiary must equal the amount shown in the accounts payable general ledger account.

**Job cost subsidiary.** One of the most important records in a home building operation, the job cost subsidiary, accumulates all construction costs: house-by-house, parcel-by-parcel, or job-by-job. This subsidiary keeps a separate account for each house, parcel, or job and classifies the costs for each house, job, or parcel into predetermined cost codes.

The operating policies and procedures of each builder, remodeler, or developer dictate the number and order of cost codes in the subsidiary ledger. The way the company estimates, purchases, and builds, remodels, or develops land should determine the number and order of cost codes. No matter how the job cost subsidiary is set up, it must be coordinated and integrated with estimating, purchasing, and scheduling to increase efficiency. Reports from the job cost subsidiary can provide builders, remodelers, and developers with cost breakdowns that enable them to control each cost; improve gross margins; and make timely decisions on product mix, marketability, and future pricing (see Chapter 9).

At the end of each month, the bookkeeper uses the job cost subsidiary to prepare a schedule showing cost to date for each unit under construction. The total construction cost from all those units must equal the balance shown in the direct construction cost account in the general ledger.

## Data Processing

When bookkeepers for builders, remodelers, and developers are processing data, they need to follow standard procedures to ensure accuracy and reliability. The following paragraphs describe how to correctly process the financial data.

### Journalizing

The first step in processing financial data is *journalizing*. The bookkeeper enters daily data into the chronological journals as he or she receives information on financial transactions.

As a control, computerized accounting systems generally do not allow an entry to be completed until debits equal credits for each transaction. In a manual system, prior to posting, the bookkeeper must ensure that the journals balance (debits equal credits).

After posting, the bookkeeper calculates new balances for each general ledger account and prepares a trial balance to ensure that debits equal credits. Even if debits equal credits, bookkeepers need to be sure that the amounts were posted to the right accounts.

Accounting software has eliminated posting as a separate step. Instead as the bookkeeper records transactions into the journals, the computer automatically completes the posting. Because many computerized systems will not allow a transaction to be processed if it is not balanced (Debits = Credits), these computer systems have eliminated human errors in transferring numbers from journals to ledger accounts.

### Adjusting Entries

At the end of each month, the accountant enters adjustments and reviews the trial balance before preparing the financial statements. Typical adjustments record depreciation of fixed assets, amortization of intangible assets (such as organization costs), and allocation of indirect construction costs between costs of sales and inventory. The accountant may make adjustments monthly, quarterly, biannually, or annually. While making adjustments, the accountant also will correct mistakes and miscoding of data.

### Closing Entries

At the end of an accounting year, the accountant prepares closing entries. These tries summarize in the owners' equity account the net income or net loss for the year. The accountant transfers the balances of the revenue and expense accounts to owners' equity. This transfer leaves the revenue and expense accounts with zero balances to start the new accounting year. Revenue and expense accounts then accumulate only the amounts for the new period. The accountant generally prepares closing entries as part of reviewing, closing, and preparing financial and managerial reports for the accounting period just ended. Computerized systems automatically do the closing entries when prompted at the end of each accounting period.

## Office Procedures

Retrieval time is a top priority in creating a filing system for a building, remodeling, or development business. Organize job documents using more than one file folder and then classify paperwork into logical groups such as permits, correspondence, customer selections, and purchase orders.

Color tabs help identify the different files, and numbers identify all files relating to a particular job. For example, if job 5412 has four file folders, all four files would have a tab with the number 5412 in addition to the name describing the types of documents in each file. Each color tab would indicate one of the following types of files:

- Red         Permits
- Blue        Correspondence
- Green       Customer selections
- Orange      Purchase orders

Organizing a filing system for invoices from trade contractors and suppliers also improves efficiency.

A number of activities in a building, remodeling, or land development firm may require separate sets of files. For example, invoices from trade contractors and suppliers generally require two filing systems: one for open or unpaid invoices and one for paid invoices.

How to file unpaid invoices depends on how the company processes payments. Draw requests for each house, remodeling job, or lot some times require copies of invoices. Group these invoices by job until draws are processed and invoices are paid. Also keep other invoices in alphabetical files until you process and pay them.

For paid invoices maintain a separate file folder for each vendor, trade contractor, or supplier, and file each invoice (with a copy of the payment check attached) in reverse chronological order in each vendor file. Some builders, remodelers, and developers file the vendor invoices by job, which makes the retrieval process difficult. Yet others cross file invoices by house, job, or lot number in an unnecessary duplicate effort.

Organizing a filing system for invoices from trade contractors and suppliers improves efficiency. An effective company filing system is easy to understand, simple to use, and increases efficiency.

# CHAPTER 6

# Internal Control

A company's internal control system comprises procedures to ensure that its assets are used properly and that its accounting information is accurate, reliable, and operates efficiently.

The purpose of the internal control system is to protect and control the company's resources through an established set of procedures that are designed to perceive error, waste, inefficiency, failure to adhere to policies, and fraud. In a small company in which the owner is in direct contact with all operations of the business, a formalized system of internal control might not be necessary. However, as the business expands and the owner ceases to maintain day-to-day contact with all phases of the business, creating a formal system of internal control becomes essential.

An internal control system protects a company's assets including cash inventories, equipment, and the like; ensures that accounting records are accurate and reliable; promotes operational efficiency; and encourages employees to follow established policies and procedures. Internal control extends beyond accounting to functions such as employee training, production efficiencies, and quality control.

Two departments, accounting and administration, are responsible for setting up the internal control system. Accounting is concerned primarily with protecting assets and ensuring that accounting data is reliable and accurate. Administrative controls focus on operational efficiencies and compliance with established policies and procedures that relate only indirectly to accounting.

The essential features for a sound control system in the accounting function or department include the following:

1. Segregating functional responsibilities
   a. Operations manager (authorizes transactions); custodian or asset manager (controls the cash, signs checks); and record keeper (enters transactions).
   b. Segregating these functions provides a system of checks and balances.
2. Authorizing and recording procedures
   a. Before a financial transaction is executed, the operations manager must authorize it.

   b. Accounting managers cannot authorize transactions; they can only process them and enter data in the accounting system.

   c. Periodically, the accountant reconciles the company's assets with the accounting records to verify the proper and authorized use of assets.

   d. Financial transactions must be recorded in a timely manner.

3. Adhering to sound practices in performing duties

   a. Standard policies and procedures must be in place and enforced.

4. Hiring and training competent and qualified staff

   a. Small companies could use outside professional accounting firms to handle their recordkeeping. However, they should ensure that the firm is familiar with the special requirements of home building.

   b. Another alternative for small companies is to use a qualified, in-house bookkeeper and have an outside professional accounting firm with home building experience supervise that person.

   c. Midsized companies should consider having a professionally trained accountant on staff.

## Segregation

Segregating operations, asset management, and record keeping is the essence of any internal control system because it reduces the likelihood of fraud, theft, or mismanagement. Nevertheless, in many small companies, fully segregating these functions is not possible. In either case, explore the possibility of insuring or bonding employees who have easy access to assets, can authorize financial transactions, and have access to the accounting records.

## Authorization

All financial transactions require proper authorization and should clearly identify the person responsible for each transaction. Therefore, the owner must delegate authority to the managers to authorize transactions and must clearly define the scope of their authority. Some companies, especially large ones, may have different levels of authority. For instance, a superintendent may spend up to $500 for extra materials and/or labor, but someone else (such as the owner or construction manager) would have to approve a larger purchase.

## Record Keeping

Recording financial transactions in the accounting system is known as record keeping. The person in charge of the record keeping should have no authority to purchase or authorize financial transactions. Employees authorizing financial transactions also should *not* have access to the accounting records. Experience shows that builders, remodelers, and developers tend to be too lax in providing adequate security for their accounting records.

Computers allow employees, even clients, trade contractors, and vendors easy access to information. Technology also can provide walls that limit access to information or block access entirely to prevent unauthorized employees from entering or changing information. The owners are responsible for developing plans for levels of access and protecting confidential data. The owner should ensure that passwords are used and changed periodically including when employees leave or new hires begin work.

## Custodianship

A custodian directly supervises the assets of the company, but the custodian should never have access to the company records or the power to authorize use of assets. The custodian allows only authorized personnel to use the assets. For example, one employee (possibly an administrative assistant) should have possession of expensive power tools the company owns (for example, a reciprocating saw); check them out only to authorized personnel; keep track of who has each tool; and make sure the borrowers return the tools in good condition.

To safeguard the company's cash, the owner must segregate authorization of transactions, record keeping, and custodianship. In a small company, the owner should maintain custodianship of the cash by retaining signature privileges for all bank accounts and by reviewing monthly bank statements. If this overview becomes too cumbersome or time consuming, the owner could choose to have two signatures on the checks and assign that task to more than one employee. Owners should bond employees who have signature privileges or who work in the accounting department.

## Policies and Procedures

The quality of a company's employees greatly impacts the success of an internal control system. But no matter how competent they are, employees must be well trained and supervised. Standardizing and documenting the internal control system's policies and procedures assures consistency and uniformity. Owners and managers must meet the challenge of updating policies and procedures as required by changes in the industry or by business expansion, contraction, or innovation. They also must ensure that employees have easy access to the latest written version of the policies and procedures. Technology allows companies to maintain electronic read-only files of policies and procedures and permit only authorized employees to change and update these documents. Using passwords for employees provides added protection by limiting their access only to electronic files that relate to job responsibilities and tasks.

Authorization procedures must clearly identify each step, as well as the employee responsible for authorizing each type of financial transaction. For instance, before paying invoices, a field employee must verify the delivery and condition of materials, completion of work, and quality. An accountant or CPA periodically may review the accounting processes and documents to ensure that the company and its employees are following proper procedures.

The owner or a top manager is responsible for designing and implementing an internal control system. The following factors influence the types and scope of control procedures a particular company requires.

## Size

The size of a company and the number of employees helps determine the internal control system. As a company expands, the owner or a top manager needs to define the span of authority for each employee, as well as each employee's place in the organizational structure. Even though authority to perform a function might be delegated to an employee, his or her supervisor (and ultimately the owner) is still responsible for the company's financial status. Therefore, the builder, remodeler, or developer must establish and follow policies and procedures to ensure that all operations are carried out properly.

As a company expands, its organizational structure becomes more complex, and it requires a more structured and detailed internal control system. In small companies in which adequate segregation of functions might prove impossible, builders, remodelers, and developers need to understand the risk of delegating more than one of the basic accounting functions (record keeping, custodianship, and authorization of transactions) to the same employee. Potential for fraud or misappropriation of assets increases as the owner delegates more than one of these functions to a single individual. The owner should bond the employee to insure against any losses caused by theft or fraud.

## Management Style

The owner's management style also plays a role in internal control procedures. Obviously, hands-on involvement produces the tightest control, but it limits the growth potential of the company. As the owner begins to delegate authority to employees, he or she simultaneously needs to increase and standardize procedures to maintain adequate operational control. Delegation does not mean abdication: As the owner delegates authority to employees, the owner also needs to hold employees accountable for their performance.

## Cost

Evaluate the cost of a procedure against its benefits. When the cost exceeds the benefits, explore alternatives and either eliminate the procedure or try a different approach. Define and validate the objective of the procedure; then simplify the process as much as possible without impairing the objective.

## Method of Collecting Financial Information

Computers have made segregation of the bookkeeping function more difficult because one employee enters data in both the general and the subsidiary ledgers. In addition, all journals and ledgers are stored on the same disk space, which can provide the bookkeeper with easy access to all records. To safe guard accounting data, use passwords to permit or restrict access to accounting files.

In addition to the broad internal control system, builders, remodelers, or developers must establish policies and procedures to maintain proper control of the following five basic business activities:

- Sales (accumulated actual sales, deposits, and cash received at contract and during the construction process; change orders that increase the original sales contract amount; and cash receipts at closing or final settlement)
- Purchasing (ordering materials or services, payables, and payment of invoices or purchase orders)

- Production and inventories (construction process and inventory management, including materials and unsold houses)
- Personnel and payroll (procedures to calculate, approve, and disburse paychecks to all employees)
- Property, plant, and equipment maintenance (overseeing use of all property and equipment owned by the company)

## Cash Management and Control

Cash management requires special attention, not just because cash is quite elusive, but also because a company cannot operate without an adequate supply of cash. The owner needs to both protect cash on hand and guard the ability to borrow cash. Therefore, builders, remodelers, or developers must pay special attention to their companies' cash needs. The owner also should set up guidelines for handling cash receipts and disbursements. This section outlines specific guidelines and procedures to help builders, remodelers, and developers safeguard the company's cash.

## Checking Account Procedures

An important element of cash control is having procedures in place that guide the accounting staff in handling and managing the company's checking account.

### Cash Balance Control

A bookkeeper usually maintains the cash balance in either the check register or on the check stubs (if checks are not drafted on the computer). A check register lists checks written and deposits made into the bank account. The register should also include all debits and credits issued by the bank, such as service charges and interest earned. Adding or subtracting these debits and credits after every transaction maintains a correct cash balance. Computer systems will maintain a detailed check register with a running cash balance that adjusts each time the bookkeeper processes deposits and drafts checks.

### Deposits

Builders, remodelers, or developers should establish a written policy to require all cash and checks received to be deposited into the company's bank account promptly. Owners should identify who is responsible for receiving the cash, preparing the deposit, and taking the deposit to the bank. Owners or top managers also must establish procedures for entering the cash received into the accounting system and filing the supporting documents.

### Withdrawals

Designated staff members should use checks for cash withdrawals and identify on the check the payee and the reason for the disbursement. Company policy should prohibit checks written to "Cash." Designated staff should only draft checks if an employee outside of the accounting department (with the known authority to do so) has duly authorized the payments. Accounting or bookkeeping staff should never initiate a payment without proper authorization.

Before paying for construction materials and labor verify price, acceptance of the materials delivered, and completion of the work done. A computer-based or manual purchase order system automatically verifies price and leaves the field superintendent responsible for verifying accurate delivery of materials and the completion of work to established quality standards. The right to approve or deny payment provides the superintendent with the authority needed to manage field work. This authority is similar to having signature privileges. Therefore, if a superintendent or anyone else approves payment prior to work being done to established quality standards, that person should face significant consequences.

When no purchase order system or estimate is in place, accounting must verify the price by referring back to purchase and trade contractor agreements. If such agreements do not exist, the company is at the mercy of trades and suppliers. Lacking such agreements strongly restricts the company's ability to control costs. A manager outside of the accounting department, typically the person that orders the materials and labor, must review the request for payment (invoice) and approve prices.

Even in large companies, check signing should remain the responsibility of the owner or treasurer. In businesses with more than one principal or partner, a two-signature requirement is common. Although requiring two signatures provides checks and balances, it also lengthens the check-writing process. The person signing checks must review supporting documentation, validate the payee, and verify the check sequence. The signer(s) of the check must review those items in greater detail, look for anything uncommon, unfamiliar, large sums, and Post Office Box addresses (that are commonly used to divert funds to illegal payees). The signer might require additional documentation before signing the check.

Companies commonly use electronic signatures or stamped signatures for signing checks. If yours does, ensure that only the appropriate employees have access to the signature mechanisms and that the signatures are kept locked up when they are not in use. Bonding everyone with signature privileges (as well as the accounting personnel) is a practical option, and it is relatively inexpensive for the protection it provides.

### Numerical Sequence of Checks

Prenumbered checks ensure accountability of all cash disbursements. Record voided checks in the check register, identify them as voided, cut off the signature area of the check, and file the voided checks. A quick review of the numerical sequence in the check register will verify that all checks have been accounted for. This practice also helps ensure that the bookkeeper has recorded all withdrawals and deducted them from the cash balance.

Avoid allowing blank checks to leave the office. All payments should originate at the company's office and preferably be drafted electronically. If taking a blank check out of the office becomes necessary record the check number, the name of the person given the check, and the reason for taking the check in a special register to facilitate follow-up. Record the transaction in the system as soon as possible.

Discourage the common practice of preparing manual checks when disbursements are required between the regular electronic check runs. When they must be written, have policies and procedures about who can prepare a manual check, who will enter it into the system, and when.

Only one person should be responsible for the blank check stock, which should be kept locked up. That person should be accountable for the proper use of all manual checks.

### Bank Reconciliation

This procedure helps control and manage cash by verifying the accuracy of the cash balance, deposits, checks, and other debits and credits shown in the company's books and the bank's records. To establish checks and balances in the cash management process, the same person who processes payables and runs checks should not do the bank reconciliation. For a small company, a sound procedure would be to have the outside accountant do the monthly bank reconciliation. In a large company, the bank reconciliation should be done by the controller or chief financial officer (CFO), never by the accounts payable clerk or person drafting the checks.

The bank usually provides a form for reconciliation of the check register with the bank statement, and many computerized accounting systems have simplified the process.

To carry out a manual reconciliation, follow these procedures:

1. Gather the previous month's reconciliation, current bank statement, canceled checks, other documentation included with the bank statement, and check register or check stubs.
2. Verify deposits shown in the check register with those shown on the bank statement.
3. List deposits made after the closing date of the bank statement.
4. Organize canceled checks numerically.
5. Compare canceled checks to the list of outstanding checks on the previous month's bank reconciliation, and list current outstanding checks.
6. Compare amounts on canceled checks with amounts recorded in the check register. Put a check mark by the verified, recorded amounts. Specifically watch for mistakes in the last two digits, or transposition of numbers. Keep in mind that banks can make mistakes when processing checks.
7. List outstanding checks for the period.
8. List and analyze charges or credits issued by the bank that are not recorded in the check register.
9. Prepare a reconciliation statement as shown in figure 6.1.

The reconciliation statement should list the following items:

- account balance
- outstanding deposits
- outstanding checks
- check register balance
- credits or charges made by the bank, but not previously recorded in the check register

If any bank charge, credit, or other transaction is not yet recorded in the accounting system, prepare a journal entry to record it.

**Figure 6.1** Bank reconciliation statement January 31, 20__

| | |
|---|---|
| Bank balance | $21,489.10 |
| Plus deposits in transit | 1,349.00 |
| Total | $22,838.10 |
| Less outstanding checks | 536.50 |
| Adjusted bank balance | $22,301.60* |
| Balance in check register | 22,421.60 |
| Credits issued by bank | 0.00 |
| Charges issued by bank | |
| Check order—printing | 105.00 |
| Service charge | 15.00 |
| Adjusted balance in check register | $22,301.60* |

List of outstanding checks

| Check number | Amount |
|---|---|
| 1031 | $151.00 |
| 1042 | 24.50 |
| 1043 | 361.00 |
| Total | $536.50 |

*The adjusted bank balance and the adjusted balance in the check register must be equal if the account is to be reconciled.

In case of a discrepancy between the bank statement and the check register balance, regardless of whether it is a manual or automated reconciliation, take the following steps:

1. Confirm that old outstanding checks have been included in the list of outstanding checks.
2. Verify amounts written on checks, specifically manual checks, against amounts posted in the check register.
3. Verify the amount shown on each check against the amount shown on the bank statement.
4. Check for transposition of numbers.
5. Identify deposits in transit.
6. Check for unexpected bank credits or charges.
7. Check for duplicate entries in the check register or bank statement.
8. Verify that all deposits have been credited to the right account and are shown in the bank statement. This error often occurs when a business has more than one account with the same bank.
8. If you are doing a manual process, check for mathematical errors.

Although the preceding list contains some of the most common causes for discrepancies, it is by no means complete. After the reconciliation, the bank balance and the balance in the accounting records must be the same. If they are not, call the company's accountant or enlist the help of the bank bookkeeping staff.

## Cash Receipts and Disbursements

The control function safeguards the company's cash through proper administration and use of the firm's cash resources. You must establish procedures to ensure the following:

- All money received is properly accounted for.
- Enough cash is available to make necessary disbursements.
- Disbursements are legitimate, necessary, and properly authorized.
- The checking account contains no idle, excess cash.

To prevent misappropriation of funds, kickbacks, and rerouting of checks, delegate authority carefully. To provide a system of checks and balances, assign different individuals to perform each of the following functions whenever possible, or consider insuring or bonding anyone who handles more than one of these tasks:

- receiving and safeguarding cash
- purchasing materials and services
- recording transactions
- approving disbursements
- signing checks

Check signers should follow these steps:

1. Review supporting documents, such as invoices, purchase orders, and statements.
2. Verify that the payee is correct and determine whether the check is to be sent to the address on the invoice. If it is not, find out why.
3. Verify payees and the amounts of checks if they are payments without invoices, such as checks for payroll, rent, and travel advances.
4. Account for all checks by reviewing their numerical sequence.
5. Generally ascertain that disbursements are reasonable.
6. Make sure that checks are distributed either through the mail or in person by someone other than the one drafting the checks.

After making disbursements, mark supporting documents as "Paid" to avoid inadvertently repaying them. File paid invoices alphabetically by vendor to facilitate retrieval and provide a record of transactions with each vendor.

## Petty Cash

A company may require a petty cash fund. It must be used strictly for small disbursements, and receipts must always substantiate these transactions.

Follow these procedures for setting up and controlling a petty cash fund:

1. Establish the fund with a check for $100 to $200, payable to Petty Cash and the person who will handle the cash.
2. Cash the check.
3. Disburse the money as necessary and replace the cash with receipts. Available cash plus receipts on hand must always equal the original petty cash fund balance.
4. When the fund needs to be replenished, draft a check payable to Petty Cash and the person handling the cash for the total amount of receipts to restore the fund to its original balance.
5. Mark "Paid" on petty cash receipts that are reimbursed by the fund. This practice prevents fraudulent reuse of the receipts.

## Loan Administration

Proper administration of loans ensures smooth disbursements of loan funds and helps maintain cooperative working relationships with lenders. Administering a loan haphazardly can jeopardize those relationships.

### Delegate Responsibility

As the first step in administering a loan, delegate the responsibility to one employee. This person must become familiar with the requirements and covenants in the loan agreements and also incorporate key dates in an electronic or manual tickler file to ensure the company meets established datelines.

### Learn and Follow Procedures

The second step is to understand and follow disbursement procedures. The person who administers the loans is responsible for contacting the lender for instructions because loan documents typically do not outline disbursement procedures. Instructions may include the answers to the following questions:

- How often will the bank make disbursements (monthly, semimonthly, weekly)?
- What is the lead time from submission of an application for a draw to disbursement?
- What are the bottleneck dates (the dates when most other borrowers are submitting their draws, and lead times for the bank to issue funds tend to be longer)?
- What format will the bank want the company to use, and does it require a special form?
- What documentation does the company need to supply: surveys, engineering reports, copies of invoices, and the like?

Each financial institution has slightly different requirements and each type of loan has different disbursement procedures. Even when renewing a loan with the same financial institution, review disbursement procedures to ensure that they have not changed.

Timely receipt of funds is a key to the smooth operation of a business. Presentation of the request for funds or draws is almost as important as the presentation to obtain the loan. If the lender requires copies of invoices as part of the draw request, make sure all copies are legible and that the invoices follow the same order in which they appear on the loan request form. Preferably, fill out the forms in the draw request package on the computer and make sure the package is clean, well organized, and professional looking. Today's technology allows for automating the reports required by lenders through the use of special report writer software.

### Account for the Funds

The third step in loan administration is to maintain accountability of the funds. In the NAHB Chart of Accounts, 1260 (due on construction and development loans), 2220 (acquisitions and development loans payable), and 2230 (construction loans payable) facilitate tracking the loan status. Signing the loan agreement establishes the obligation or liability; thus, you credit the amount of the loan to 2220 or 2230 depending on whether it is an acquisition and development loan or a construction loan. Simultaneously, debit the amount of the loan to 1260, an asset, to establish the dollars available through the loan.

Every time you take a draw, a credit to 1260 will reduce the balance available to draw on the loan. The difference between the balance to draw (1260) and the loan payable (2220 or 2230) is the total amount drawn to date, or the amount due to be paid to the lender at any given time. The balance on 1260 indicates how much is left to draw on the loan.

The loan administrator should make periodic assessments as to whether the loans will be paid on their due dates; and if not, prior to the due dates, prepare documentation, exercise extension options, or negotiate new extensions.

## Estimating and Purchasing

Estimating, purchasing, and cost control must operate under the same structure to increase efficiencies and eliminate duplication and unnecessary tasks. Estimating must match the way you purchase material and labor to eliminate the need to rearrange material lists or trade work orders. Make the purchase units match how the company will pay them so the budget or estimate amounts match the amounts to be paid and facilitate the control function. If the amounts do not match, withhold payment to the supplier or trade until you justify the discrepancy. Using the same structure in all three processes provides a direct flow of information from estimating to purchasing to accounts payable and control.

The cost control function compares projected costs or estimates and actual costs. Without a standardized structure to accumulate actual cost (job cost accounts) and prepare the estimates, you cannot make meaningful comparisons between estimates and actual costs.

Estimating, purchasing, and ordering materials and labor generally follow the construction sequence. Therefore, organize job cost accounts to also follow the construction sequence. This structure provides the necessary link to approve payments directly from the jobsite.

Information technology allows builders, remodelers, and developers to integrate estimating, purchasing, scheduling, and payable systems. This integration is commonly referred to as a paperless system. To achieve full automation, all three processes must be coordinated and use the same general structure, as discussed above. The speed, simplification, and efficiency of a paperless system are dreams come true.

The owner or construction manager releases purchase orders and schedules electronically to the trades, and the field superintendents update the schedules daily. As they update the schedules, the superintendents also are approving and releasing completed purchase orders for payment. Accounting processes payments from the approved purchase orders (not invoices) logged into the system with the option of sending payments electronically to the bank accounts of the vendors and the trades. The end of the paper chase!

## Coordination with the Accounting System

The accounting system measures and accumulates, in separate cost codes, actual costs incurred for each house during construction. A common problem in developing a job cost chart of accounts is the temptation to include too many accounts. Builders who break down cost codes into minute components end up with too much detail, which in most cases is irrelevant at the accounting level. The detail should be kept at the estimating and purchasing levels where price negotiations with trades and suppliers take place. Each cost code should represent a control point that equates to a pay point.

The following guidelines help in developing a job cost chart of accounts:

- Keep it simple. Avoid using more cost codes than you absolutely need.
- Coordinate job cost codes with estimating, purchasing, and how you pay your suppliers and trade contractors.
- Assign only one vendor to a cost code.
- Whenever possible, each cost code should represent only one purchase order or invoice. Combine orders from one vendor on one purchase order if delivery is to be made at the same time to facilitate this situation.
- Follow the construction sequence to coordinate the invoice approval process with the scheduling system.
- Make sure cost codes reflect the way you build.
- Break down cost codes into material and labor only if you are not doing turnkey contracts with the trades. Otherwise, separate the contract amount into cost codes that reflect the amounts to be paid at each draw.

Appendix E provides an example of a job cost chart of accounts. Use this example only as a general guide because each company needs to generate its own cost codes based on the guidelines outlined previously.

## Change Orders

Change orders have challenged nearly every company, primarily because of the lack of policies and procedures regarding their handling and processing. The following guidelines can help you develop your company's own policy and procedures:

- Define, in detail, company policy regarding change orders; then enforce it.

- Establish who has the authority to
    - Initiate a change order; preferably limit the authority to one person. (Do not use a field manager because processing paperwork is not usually a field manager's strength.)
    - Price a change order.
    - Issue a change order.
    - Institute and collect an administrative fee for processing a change order and to collect payment for the change order.
- Determine who needs to be notified of the change order and who will send the notices.
- Include a total contract price in the change order and carry over the adjusted contract price after processing each change order to eliminate surprises at the closing table.
- Include accounting in the notification list for each change order to ensure that the person responsible will collect the money for the change order and adjust the final contract price accordingly.

After the start of construction, change orders are disruptive to the construction process: the objective of any change order policy should be to eliminate them as much as possible. At least establish time limitations based on the stages of construction. Change orders after start of construction are generally caused by poor preconstruction processes. Review the sales and selection processes and refine the processes with the goal of providing steps and tasks to help eliminate the need for change orders.

## Payroll

Some builders, remodelers, and developers incorrectly use the term *payroll* to include payments to the trades. In this section, the term *payroll* refers to the payment of salaries and wages to company employees not trade contractors. A significant number of federal, state, county, and municipal requirements govern payroll. Regardless of the size of the company or the number of employees, payroll also requires numerous reports. Payroll service companies have streamlined the process and offer their services for reasonable fees, sometimes well below the cost to do the payroll in house. Aside from cost, using a payroll service offers numerous advantages, including confidentiality and timely reports and deposits. Many builders, remodelers, and developers, who use these services, strongly recommend them.

# CHAPTER 7

# Financial and Management Reports

Because today's financial and management reports are so easy and inexpensive to produce, building industry professionals often have difficulty culling the most important information from reams of data about their companies' performance. Beware of the potential for information overload and avoid producing unnecessary reports with too much data. Longer is not necessarily better.

How you set up a chart of accounts determines the types of reports the book-keeper or accountant is able to prepare. Therefore, consider reporting needs before creating a chart of accounts. In deciding what reports to produce, the most important criterion is their potential value in making decisions about your business. Conduct a cost-benefit analysis before preparing a special report.

Reports that compare historical data to a plan or budget, results from prior periods, or industry performance provide more information. To ensure comparability, use the same methods and procedures to accumulate data from period to period. Consider the following guidelines when preparing financial reports:

- Make reports easy to read and understand.
- Indicate the source of the data.
- Highlight any deviations from a plan or budget.
- Make actual and planned or budgeted numbers comparable.
- Generally, include more detail in reports for owners of small companies than for owners of large companies. In large companies detailed reports go to managers of specific functions or departments. The owners receive summary reports with back up data available on request.
- Issue reports in a timely manner so a builder, remodeler, or developer can take action to solve any problems the reports reveal.
- Keep information relevant, accurate, and reliable.
- Use standardized formats whenever possible.

# Balance Sheet and Income Statement

To prepare a balance sheet and an income statement, group the balances in the general ledger accounts into the standard GAAP formats. Comparing current results with data for prior periods and with industry standards makes these reports more useful. In addition, calculating financial ratios can enhance the usefulness of financial information presented on these two reports.

Using the accounting equations simplifies the balance sheet and the income statement as follows:

### Balance Sheet

Assets = Liabilities + Owners' equity

### Income Statement

Revenues – Cost and expenses = Net income or net loss

The net income or loss appears in the balance sheet in the owners' equity section under retained earnings.

### *Balance Sheet*

The balance sheet represents a company's financial position on a specific date: generally the end of a month, quarter, or year (fig. 7.1). It reflects the value of a firm's assets on a cost or market basis, and it identifies who has claims to the assets (creditors or owners) and the amounts of those claims.

Each financial transaction affects a company's financial condition. Therefore, the balance sheet (a static report) is current only as of the date indicated on it.

Builders, remodelers, and developers use the balance sheet primarily to evaluate a company's financial strength, liquidity, and leverage. The balance sheet provides general information for developing company plans and goals, and it offers information to potential lenders and investors for evaluating the risk factor for loans and investments.

A trend (or comparative) analysis of more than one balance sheet can help identify the company's overall operating philosophy, structural changes, and liquidity patterns. Examined in conjunction with the income statement, a balance sheet reveals other important information, such as how effectively a company uses its resources, the status of investments in land and inventories, the rate of return on assets and owners' equity, and leverage. Chapter 8 discusses financial analysis and ratios in more detail.

**Assets.** A company's assets are items of value that it owns (such as cash, equipment, and land), or they may be claims or future benefits (such as prepaid insurance, accounts receivable, and other prepaid expenses).

Assets generally are represented by debit balances in the accounting system. Therefore, a debit entry increases the asset while a credit entry decreases the asset. The NAHB Chart of Accounts (Appendix B) identifies assets in the 1000 series.

**Liabilities.** Obligations to third parties, such as accounts payable, loans payable, and payroll taxes payable are liabilities. They represent claims to the firm's assets by outsiders.

**Figure 7.1** Balance sheet

**XYZ Home Building Company**
**Balance Sheet**
**December 31, 20__**

**Assets**

Current assets

| | | |
|---|---|---|
| Cash | $ 985,000 | |
| Inventories Land | 10,200,000 | |
| Inventories Houses | 4,500,000 | |
| Total current assets | 15,685,000 | |
| Other assets net of depreciation | 1,450,000 | |
| Total assets | $17,135,000 | |

**Liabilities and Owner's Equity**

Liabilities

| | | |
|---|---|---|
| Current liabilities | $ 9,200,000 | |
| Long-term liabilities | 4,300,000 | |
| Total liabilities | | 13,500,000 |
| Owners' equity | | |
| Invested capital | $ 2,500,000 | |
| Retained earnings | 1,135,000 | |
| Total owners' equity | | 3,635,000 |
| Total liabilities and owners' equity | | $17,135.000 |

The accounting system represents liabilities with credit balances. Therefore, a debit to a liability account decreases the liability, whereas a credit increases the liability. The chart of accounts identifies liabilities by the 2000 series.

**Owners' equity.** Capital contributions that owners have invested in the company appear in the chart of accounts as owners' equity. They are claims of the owners on the company's assets.

Owners' equity has two components: the owners' investment (invested capital or capital stock) and retained earnings (the accumulation of profits or losses from operations). On a balance sheet, the retained earnings account reflects the firm's net profit or loss accumulated from the time the business was established, less any dividends paid to the owners or cash withdrawals made by the owners.

Owners' equity accounts usually carry a credit balance unless these accounts show a deficit; then a debit balance would represent the owners' equity accounts. The NAHB Chart of Accounts also identifies owners' equity accounts in the 2000 series along with the liabilities.

## Income Statement

For a stated period of time, such as a month, quarter, or year, the income statement summarizes revenues, cost of sales, and operating expenses. The net income or net loss on the statement reflects the result of the company's operations for the period specified (fig. 7.2). Net profit or net loss increases or decreases the owners' equity for the period on the balance sheet. Thus, the net profit or net loss keeps the accounting equation in balance.

### Revenues

Revenues are represented by credit balances in the accounting system because they increase the owners' equity. These accounts represent the monetary consideration received or earned by providing goods and services to a third party.

Revenues are usually presented as a lump sum on the income statement. However, if your business provides more than one type of product or service, you should identify each source of revenue. Some examples follow:

■ sales of single-family speculative homes
■ sales of single-family, custom-designed homes
■ sales of developed lots
■ remodeling
■ rental of construction equipment

**Figure 7.2** Income statement

**XYZ Home Building Company**
**Income Statement**
**For the year ended December 31, 20__**

**Revenues**

| | | |
|---|---:|---:|
| Sales—single family | | $29,650,000 |
| Cost of sales: | | |
| Land | $ 3,700,000 | |
| Direct construction cost | 17,150,000 | |
| Total cost of sales | | 20,850,000 |
| Gross profit | | $ 8,800,000 |
| **Operating Expenses** | | |
| Indirect construction cost | 860,000 | |
| Financing expenses | 1,560,000 | |
| Sales and marketing expenses | 2,200,000 | |
| General and administrative expenses | 1,425,000 | |
| Total operating expenses | | 6,045,000 |
| Net profit | | $ 2,755,000 |

If you combine different types of revenues, you cannot easily analyze how well each revenue center performed, and identifying functions that need improvement is difficult.

### Cost of Sales

Use the cost of sales account for costs associated with the products your business sells. Cost adds value to the product. In contrast, although expenses are necessary for the day-to-day operation of a business, they do not add value to a product.

In a home building, remodeling, or land development operation, cost of sales accounts include cost of land, land development, and construction. Typically, accountants divide construction cost into two major categories: direct construction cost (materials and labor) and indirect construction cost (costs associated with the building process).

**Direct construction cost.** These accounts (in NAHB's 1410 and 1430 series) include the cost of the sticks and bricks and construction labor. A builder, remodeler, or developer can trace a direct cost to a particular project, unit of construction, remodeling job, or parcel of land.

**Indirect construction cost.** These indirect cost accounts (in the 4000 series) include costs incurred during construction that cannot be directly assigned to a particular unit of construction. Examples of indirect construction cost include supervision, field offices, operation of construction vehicles, warehousing of construction materials, and temporary utilities.

Sometimes builders, remodelers, and developers use the term *overhead* to describe this type of cost (see the cautions in Chapter 4).

**Absorption costing.** This method of costing requires including both direct and indirect costs in the total cost of each unit of production. Because indirect construction costs do not relate directly to a unit of production, allocate a proportional share of the cost to each unit, job, or lot. Absorption costing combines the proportional share of indirect construction cost for the unit, job, or lot with its direct construction cost to determine the total cost of the unit, job, or lot. Indirect construction costs accumulate in inventory account 1440, an asset. This account requires a subsidiary account to track each specific type of cost in this major classification. This subsidiary ledger operates as other subsidiaries do in the accounting system.

GAAP and the IRS require valuing inventories and cost of sales according to the absorption costing method. However, consider an alternate method to track and control indirect construction costs. Instead of accumulating the indirect costs in an inventory (asset) account with a subsidiary, treat them as operating expenses and accumulate them in the 4000 series of accounts. This practice facilitates evaluating each type of cost. Owners and managers then can control these expenses as part of the general ledger and eliminate the need for a subsidiary ledger.

They then can track and analyze the indirect construction costs associated with production as they do the finance, sales and marketing, and administrative costs. However, when you set up your accounting system this way remember to comply with external reporting requirements and IRS regulations. Allocate the proportional amount of the cost in the 4000 series that relates to the work-in-progress inventory to an inventory account (1440). This allocation does not require a detailed breakdown of the types of costs because the system maintains the detail in the 4000 series. Your accountant can easily make this adjustment at the end of each accounting period.

### *Allocation of Indirect Construction Costs*

Based on projected production for the year, prepare a budget or plan for indirect costs to be incurred during the accounting year for a total budgeted indirect cost. Based upon projected sales for the same period, estimate the number of units, jobs, or lots to be built or developed for the anticipated level of production.

Measure the level of production in different ways, including number of units, dollar amount of direct construction cost, or direct labor hours. Each method has its advantages and drawbacks so select a method that best suits your company's way of doing business. For example, a production builder or a developer might express production level by number of units or lots. To allocate indirect costs as construction or development progresses, divide the budgeted indirect costs by the number of units or lots the company expects to produce and the result is the amount of indirect costs to charge to each of the units or lots as follows:

| | |
|---|---|
| Projected indirect cost for the year | $525,000 |
| Projected volume in units | 250 |
| Allocation per unit ($525,000 / 250) | $ 2,100 |

Under this method, you would add the indirect construction cost of $2,100 to the cost of sale for each house or lot sold during the year. Because the allocation rate is typically based on estimates, the allocated amount will probably not exactly match the actual cost. At year-end, the accountant or CPA will reconcile the actual cost to the allocated amount.

In a business with a diversified product line, such as a builder who also does some remodeling, distribution of indirect construction cost to units or jobs using the same dollar amount would not be equitable. Large projects take longer to build so they bear a larger share of indirect construction cost. For businesses with their own crews, expressing production level by labor hours or direct construction cost provides a more effective way of allocating the indirect construction cost.

In the example presented below, for each dollar of direct construction cost add 3.3 cents of indirect construction cost to the unit cost as follows:

| | |
|---|---|
| Projected indirect construction cost | $525,000 |
| Projected direct construction cost | $15,750,000 |
| Ratio of $525,000 ÷ $15,750,000 | 3.3% |

The larger or more costly the house, remodeling job, or developed lot, the larger the share of indirect cost as the following two examples illustrate:

#### Model A, Unit 205

| | |
|---|---|
| Cost of land | $ 18,000 |
| Direct construction cost | 95,500 |
| Indirect construction cost of 3.3% | 3,151 |
| Total cost of house | $116,651 |

**Model B, Unit 125**

| | |
|---|---|
| Cost of land | $ 25,250 |
| Direct construction cost | 115,950 |
| Indirect construction cost of 3.3% | 3,826 |
| Total cost of house | $145,026 |

Allocating indirect construction costs is not required on an ongoing basis, particularly when you use the 4000 series of accounts to track these costs. Allocation would occur on a monthly, quarterly, or annual basis or when you report to third parties that mandate using the absorption method of accounting. Generally the CPA or accountant will calculate the allocation.

In a development company, the nature and allocation of indirect construction cost would vary depending upon a project's size and duration. Large developments usually incorporate recreational facilities, open spaces, amenities, and impact fees. Developers must allocate a proportional share of the cost of these items to each lot as indirect costs. The development process also could extend beyond a year. In that case, estimating the total indirect construction cost for the entire life of the development process and dividing by the number of lots yields the proper allocation for each finished lot.

Two methods are commonly used to allocate costs. One method divides the total indirect cost by the number of finished lots and allocates the same amount to each lot. Another method uses the market value of a development to calculate a ratio. For example, if the total market value of a development is $2.5 million and the indirect costs for the project total $250,000, the ratio of indirect cost to market value is 10%. Therefore, the developer would add $2,500 of indirect costs to the cost of each lot.

Unless a remodeling company chooses to use the completed-contract method of recognizing income, it need not be concerned with the allocating indirect construction costs. For remodelers that recognize revenues as they collect on contracts, indirect construction costs become period costs that can be charged off in the period in which they are incurred. Series 4000 of the NAHB Chart of Accounts identifies indirect construction costs as period costs.

If a remodeler uses the completed-contract method (recognizing revenue only when the contract is complete), direct construction costs for a remodeling job accumulate in an inventory account until completion. At completion, the remodeler recognizes direct construction cost as cost of sales and includes a proportional share of indirect construction costs in the cost of each job. The IRS requires the company to allocate indirect construction costs to all jobs. Therefore, because the types and sizes of remodeling jobs are so diverse, the best method of allocation for remodelers is the ratio of indirect cost to total construction cost.

Chapter 15 discusses in more detail options that builders, remodelers, and developers can use to allocate indirect construction cost between cost of sales and work-in-process inventories.

## Operating Expenses

Operating expenses incurred in the day-to-day operation of a business are classified into three major categories: financing, sales and marketing, and general and administrative. Indirect construction costs are operating expenses under the direct costing method of accounting.

### Financing Expenses

A major line item in any building or development company, financing expenses, include interest, points, and fees paid in relation to borrowing or commitments to borrow money. Because building and development businesses usually operate on borrowed money, financing expenses can be significant. They include the following categories: development and construction loans, commitments for permanent financing, points, other fees paid at closings, and funds borrowed for operating capital.

Interest incurred on finished lots, completed units, or model homes can be expensed when incurred.

The process of adding construction financing expenses to the cost of units built is called *capitalization*. Accumulate and include as inventory interest paid on construction loans during construction, regardless of whether the interest relates to land development or direct construction costs. Expense interest paid on finished lots, completed units, or model homes as they occur.

Other financing expenses are treated as regular expenses, regardless of operational structure. The 5000 series of the NAHB Chart of Accounts break down financing expenses.

As with indirect construction cost, an alternate method of accounting for financing expenses helps owners and managers analyze and control them. Interim financing expenses can be accumulated in the 5000 series expense classification with an adjustment for reporting to third parties that require using capitalization. This procedure shows management the total cost of financing production for a given period.

Although interest rates are set by external economic forces over which management has little control, it can negotiate rates and terms. In addition, construction cycle time and the number of unsold finished homes strongly influences construction financing expenses. Therefore, efficient construction and development schedules help to control these expenses, as does careful management of speculative inventory. Closely monitor financing expenses so that you can adjust the pricing of products and services to reflect rate increases or decreases. Also monitor interest rates to evaluate the possibility of future growth and to determine long-range plans, future marketability, and pricing policies. As a general rule, remodelers do not carry loans on their jobs because the home owners secure any loans required.

### Sales and Marketing Expenses

A strong economy requires fewer marketing dollars, whereas hard economic times tend to require a larger share of gross margin dollars for creative marketing approaches. This group of expenses measures the effectiveness of your marketing and sales efforts. The structure of the sales and marketing function impacts the ability to control these expenses. If a company has no in-house sales force, expense is determined somewhat by the prevailing commission rate in the area. An in-house sales force allows you more control over your sales and marketing expenses as well as over the processes and procedures.

Series 6000 in the NAHB Chart of Accounts identifies sales and marketing expenses.

### General and Administrative Expenses

This category usually includes expenses related to running the office, such as salaries of administrative personnel and officers, rent, supplies, insurance, licenses, travel and entertainment, educational programs, and professional fees. Record these expenses in separate accounts to measure the effectiveness of each type. Managers can then use the account reports to make decisions to curtail or expand a particular line item. Some of these expenses may be subject to the IRS's capitalization rule so seek advice from a tax expert to make necessary adjustments when preparing your business's income tax return.

Series 8000 of the NAHB Chart of Accounts presents a detailed list of the different types of expenses classified in this series. You can expand it as necessary to meet the needs of your business.

### Other Income and Expenses

The "other" category includes items that (1) do not relate to the main economic activity of the business or (2) are for extraordinary transactions that are not part of the everyday operation of the business. One example is a gain or loss on the sale of office equipment. Series 9000 in the NAHB Chart of Accounts identifies this category.

## Enhance the Income Statement

Figures 7.3 and 7.4 illustrate how to enhance information presented in your income statement by comparing actual to budget and adding ratios in additional columns. You can further enhance the information available from your income

**Figure 7.3** Comparative income statement

| XYZ Home Building Company Income Statement For year ended December 31, 20__ | | | |
|---|---|---|---|
| **Revenues** | **Actual** | **Budget** | **Variance** |
| Sales—Single family | $29,650,000 | $32,540,000 | $2,890,000 |
| Cost of sales | | | |
| Land | 3,700,000 | 3,850,000 | 150,000 |
| Direct construction cost | 17,150,000 | 17,897,000 | 747,000 |
| Total cost of sales | 20,850,000 | 21,747,000 | 897,000 |
| Gross profit | 8,800,000 | 10,793,000 | 1,993,000 |
| | | | |
| **Operating expenses** | | | |
| Indirect construction cost | 860,000 | 875,000 | 15,000 |
| Financing expenses | 1,560,000 | 1,850,000 | 290,000 |
| Sales and marketing | 2,200,000 | 2,950,000 | 750,000 |
| General and administrative | 1,425,000 | 1,575,000 | 150,000 |
| Total operating expenses | 6,045,000 | 7,250,000 | 1,205,000 |
| | | | |
| Net profit | $ 2,755,000 | $ 3,543,000 | $ 788,000 |

**Figure 7.4** Income statement with ratios

| | | | Ratios | |
|---|---|---|---|---|
| **XYZ Home Building Company** | | | | |
| **Income Statement** | | | | |
| **For year ended December 31, 20__** | | | | |
| **Revenues** | **Actual** | **Budget** | **Actual** | **Budget** |
| Sales—single family | $29,650,000 | $32,540,000 | 100.0% | 100.0% |
| Cost of sales | | | | |
|     Land | $ 3,700,000 | $ 3,850,000 | 12.5 | 11.8 |
|     Direct construction cost | 17,150,000 | 17,897,000 | 57.8 | 55.0 |
| Total cost of sales | 20,850,000 | 21,747,000 | 70.3 | 66.8 |
| Gross profit | 8,800,000 | 10,793,000 | 29.7 | 33.2 |
| **Operating expenses** | | | | |
|     Indirect construction cost | 860,000 | 875,000 | 2.9 | 2.7 |
|     Financing expenses | 1,560,000 | 1,850,000 | 5.3 | 5.7 |
|     Sales and marketing | 2,200,000 | 2,950,000 | 7.4 | 9.1 |
|     General and administrative | 1,425,000 | 1,575,000 | 4.8 | 4.8 |
| Total operating expenses | 6,045,000 | 7,250,000 | 20.4 | 22.3 |
| Net profit | $ 2,755,000 | $ 3,543,000 | 9.3 | 10.9 |

statement by including, for example, comparisons with year-to-date numbers, prior year numbers, and industry ratios.

## Cash Flow Statement

Another important financial statement, the cash flow statement, analyzes the changes in cash during a given time period. The traditional cash flow statement is difficult to understand and follow because it does not clearly identify the sources or uses of cash. Chapter 8 discusses cash flow analysis and reporting in detail.

## Management Reports

In addition to the standard financial statements, owners and managers should receive a number of management reports on a monthly basis. Some of these reports involve accounting system data while others require information from other sources.

Make the following management reports part of the monthly financial package for owners and top managers:

- For companies with multiple projects, side-by-side *project or community income statements* highlight the contribution margin or operating profit that each project or community contributes to the business (fig. 7.5).

**Figure 7.5**  Income statements by project

| | Target | Total Company | The Meadows | River Run | The Groves | The Outlook | Meadow Hills | Sierra Run |
|---|---|---|---|---|---|---|---|---|
| | | | **Year ended December 31, 20__** | | | | | |
| Sales | 100.00% | 100.00% | 100.00% | 100.00% | 100.00% | 100.00% | 100.00% | 100.00% |
| Cost of sales | 70.00 | 76.59 | 68.14 | 84.54 | 72.82 | 81.73 | 84.95 | 79.03 |
| Gross profit | 30.00 | 23.41 | 31.86 | 15.46 | 27.18 | 18.27 | 15.05 | 20.97 |
| Operating expenses | | | | | | | | |
| Indirect construction cost | 3.50 | 6.67 | 3.21 | 4.38 | 3.60 | 1.22 | 2.44 | 5.95 |
| Sales and marketing | 6.00 | 8.57 | 3.50 | 19.18 | 8.92 | 6.95 | 2.99 | 9.54 |
| Financing | 4.00 | 4.25 | 1.12 | 3.83 | 1.37 | 0.28 | 1.74 | 0.67 |
| General & administrative | 4.50 | 9.62 | | | | | | |
| Total operating expenses | 18.00 | 29.11 | 7.83 | 27.39 | 13.89 | 8.45 | 7.17 | 16.16 |
| Operating profit | 12.00 | −5.70 | 24.03 | −11.93 | 13.29 | 9.82 | 7.88 | 4.81 |

■ The *gross profit report* sorted and totaled by community. Use one line per house to show sales price, concessions or premiums, net price, cost of lot, direct construction cost, and gross profit. The report should show the dollar amount and the percentage of each item reflected in the sales price. Every house closed during the reporting period should appear on the gross profit report to provide a quick overview of the profitability of each. If the gross profit from the house meets targets, a detailed job cost report is unnecessary. If the gross profit does not meet the goal, you should provide detailed job cost reports for further review of the jobs (figs. 7.6 and 7.7).

**Figure 7.6**  Gross profit by units

| | Unit 281 | | Unit 280 | | Unit 287 | | Unit 274 | |
|---|---|---|---|---|---|---|---|---|
| | | | **Units closed in March 20__** | | | | | |
| Sales | $199,500 | 100.00% | $382,643 | 100.00% | $379,000 | 100.00% | $449,900 | 100.00% |
| Land | $26,000 | 13.03 | $56,403 | 14.74 | $40,122 | 10.59 | $69,000 | 15.34 |
| Direct cost | $135,079 | 67.71 | $252,169 | 65.90 | $252,103 | 66.52 | $272,267 | 60.52 |
| Total cost | $161,079 | 80.74 | $308,572 | 80.64 | $292,225 | 77.10 | $341,267 | 75.85 |
| Gross profit | $38,421 | 19.26 | $74,071 | 19.36 | $86,775 | 22.90 | $108,633 | 24.15 |

**Figure 7.1** Gross profit report

**Units closed in March 20___**

**Meadow Hills Community**

| Job number | Model number | Sales price | Lot cost | % of lot costs | Direct cost | % DCC | Total cost | % total | Gross profit | % GP |
|---|---|---|---|---|---|---|---|---|---|---|
| 356 | 1850A | $175,800 | $35,000 | 19.9 | $93,600 | 53.2 | $128,600 | 73.2 | $47,200 | 26.8 |
| 361 | 2050B | $198,500 | $35,000 | 17.6 | $99,650 | 50.2 | $134,650 | 67.8 | $63,850 | 32.2 |
| 364 | 1710C | $165,750 | $35,000 | 21.1 | $87,630 | 52.9 | $122,630 | 74.0 | $43,120 | 26.0 |
| 365 | 1850A | $180,350 | $35,000 | 19.4 | $96,540 | 53.5 | $131,540 | 72.9 | $48,810 | 27.1 |
| Total | | $720,400 | $140,000 | 19.4 | $377,420 | 52.4 | $517,420 | 71.8 | $202,980 | 28.2 |

**The Falls**

| Job number | Model number | Sales price | Lot cost | % of lot costs | Direct cost | % DCC | Total cost | % total | Gross profit | % GP |
|---|---|---|---|---|---|---|---|---|---|---|
| 251 | 1970A | $235,600 | $50,000 | 21.2 | $132,200 | 56.1 | $182,200 | 77.3 | $53,400 | 22.7 |
| 263 | 2250B | $275,750 | $60,000 | 21.8 | $151,900 | 55.1 | $211,900 | 76.8 | $63,850 | 23.2 |
| 295 | 1970B | $252,300 | $50,000 | 19.8 | $132,500 | 52.5 | $182,500 | 72.3 | $69,800 | 27.7 |
| 298 | 2250C | $315,000 | $60,000 | 19.0 | $168,500 | 53.5 | $228,500 | 72.5 | $86,500 | 27.5 |
| Total | | $1,078,650 | $220,000 | 20.4 | $585,100 | 54.2 | $805,100 | 74.6 | $273,550 | 25.4 |

| Company totals | | $1,799,050 | $360,000 | 20.0 | $962,520 | 53.5 | $1,322,520 | 73.5 | $476,530 | 26.5 |
|---|---|---|---|---|---|---|---|---|---|---|

**Figure 7.8** Meadow Hills project

**Variance Report for January 20__**

| | | | | |
|---|---|---|---|---|
| Design error | 1 | 1% | $520 | 1% |
| Estimate change/error | 20 | 6 | 1,780 | 3 |
| Site condition | 50 | 14 | 10,986 | 21 |
| Equipment rental | 1 | 0 | 54 | 0 |
| Back charge | 42 | 12 | 314 | 1 |
| Theft, vandalism | 28 | 8 | 2,521 | 5 |
| Rework and repair | 25 | 7 | 3,548 | 7 |
| Sales concession | 8 | 2 | 888 | 2 |
| Code change | 5 | 1 | 282 | 1 |
| Trade contractors error | | 0 | | 0 |
| Weather conditions | 4 | 1 | 278 | 1 |
| Vendor error | 2 | 1 | −21 | −0 |
| Purchasing change/error | 66 | 19 | 8,935 | 17 |
| PO not issued | 100 | 28 | 21,422 | 41 |
| Total | 352 | 100% | $51,507 | 100% |

■ Prepare *cost variance reports* showing variances by reason, vendor, job, and other criteria of value to your company. Top management, production management, purchasing, estimating, and superintendents should all review cost variance reports regularly with the objective of eradicating variances.

## Other Reports

Aside from accounting, other company functions also need to track information and prepare management reports. The sales and marketing function or department must track traffic, conversion rates (traffic units divided by net contracts), gross sales, cancellations, net sales, and closings. Production should track starts, closings, construction schedules, and warranty items.

## Charts and Graphs

Charts and graphs help users interpret the reports. Builders, remodelers, and developers are used to reading blueprints; therefore, they relate well to charts and graphs. The following charts provide examples of how gross profit, variances, and warranty information translate to charts and graphs (figs. 7.9–7.14). Software programs allow easy and quick production of charts.

**Figure 7.9**  Percentage of gross profit per unit

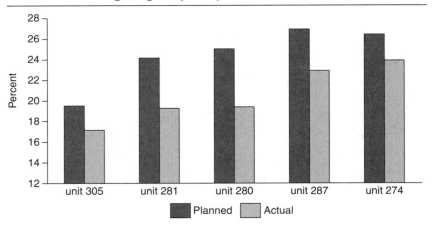

**Figure 7.10**  Percentage of gross profit by project

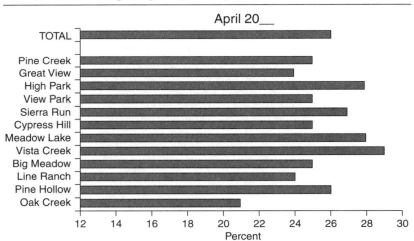

**Figure 7.11**  Percentage of variances by project

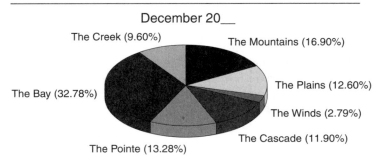

**Figure 7.12**  Meadow Hill project

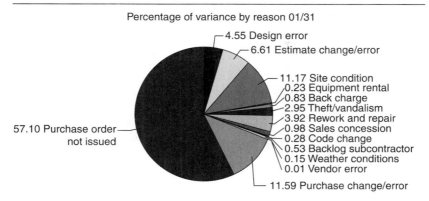

Percentage of variance by reason 01/31

4.55 Design error
6.61 Estimate change/error
11.17 Site condition
0.23 Equipment rental
0.83 Back charge
2.95 Theft/vandalism
3.92 Rework and repair
0.98 Sales concession
0.28 Code change
0.53 Backlog subcontractor
0.15 Weather conditions
0.01 Vendor error
57.10 Purchase order not issued
11.59 Purchase change/error

**Figure 7.13**  Month-to-date variance totals

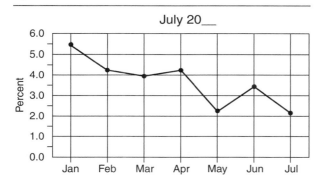

July 20__

**Figure 7.14**  Percentage of warranty expense

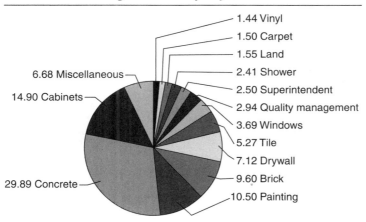

1.44 Vinyl
1.50 Carpet
1.55 Land
2.41 Shower
2.50 Superintendent
2.94 Quality management
3.69 Windows
5.27 Tile
7.12 Drywall
9.60 Brick
10.50 Painting
6.68 Miscellaneous
14.90 Cabinets
29.89 Concrete

# CHAPTER 8

# Financial Analysis

The analytical review of the financial information accumulated in the accounting system and reported in the financial statements is called a *financial analysis*. It helps identify trends and compare the data in the financial reports with predetermined goals, industry standards, and data from prior periods. These comparisons enable the builder, remodeler, and developer to measure their businesses' financial strength, operational efficiency, and return on investment. Financial analysis allows owners and managers to isolate problems or functions that need improvement. It also helps business owners to achieve the ultimate goal of maximizing profits in the long term and obtaining the best return on investment.

This chapter discusses specifically how financial analysis can help builders, remodelers, and developers can improve their business operations.

## Gross Profit Analysis

The difference between sales and cost of sales is gross profit. In the following equation, cost of sales includes only lot and direct construction costs:

$$\text{Gross profit} = \text{Sales} - \text{Cost of sales}$$

To obtain a gross profit ratio, divide sales into gross profit as follows:

$$\text{Gross profit ratio} = \frac{\text{Gross profit}}{\text{Sales}}$$

Gross profit is the first line of defense against poor financial performance. If a builder, remodeler, or developer does not attain an adequate gross profit ratio, his or her likelihood of obtaining strong net profits greatly declines.

Looking at gross profit per model, unit, remodeling job, or lot shows the contribution that each model, unit, remodeling job, or lot makes toward company operating expenses and profit (fig. 8.1).

**Figure 8.1** Gross profit per model, unit, remodeling job, or lot

| **Mocdel A** | |
| --- | --- |
| Sales price | $255,000 |
| Cost of sales | − 178,500 |
| Gross profit | = $ 76,500 |
| | |
| Gross profit ratio | $76,500 ÷ $ 255,000 = 30% |

Comparing the gross profit of different models, units, jobs, or lots provides builders with information to make decisions about product mix and pricing (fig. 8.2).

Remodelers and developers can also use gross profit analysis. The higher the gross profit ratio among remodeling jobs and land parcels, the greater the potential for net profit.

Two factors affect gross profit: sales price and cost of sales. The local market generally sets the sales price, and often a builder, remodeler, or developer has little room to increase prices to improve the gross profit ratio without affecting the sales velocity (the number of units that can be sold in a given time period). Only if the sales price is below market, can a builder, remodeler, or developer increase the gross profit ratio by raising the sales price and not significantly impact sales velocity.

On the other hand, reducing cost of sales (lot cost and direct cost) and, specifically, direct construction cost, presents the greatest potential for increasing gross profit. Controlling direct construction costs starts with efficient designs and accu-

**Figure 8.2** Gross profit by product mix and pricing

| | **Model B** | **Model C** | **Model D** | **Total** |
| --- | --- | --- | --- | --- |
| Sales price | $174,500 | $199,750 | $215,000 | |
| Cost of sales | 135,412 | 147,416 | 161,680 | |
| Gross profit | $ 39,088 | $ 52,334 | $ 53,320 | |
| Gross profit ratio | 22.4% | 26.2% | 24.8% | |
| Units sold | 5 | 2 | 3 | 10 |
| Gross profit by model | $195,440 | $104,668 | $159,960 | $460,068 |
| | | | | |
| A change in product mix produces different results as follows: | | | | |
| | | | | |
| Units sold | 3 | 4 | 3 | 10 |
| Gross profit by model | $117,264 | $209,336 | $159,960 | $486,560 |

Changing the product mix to 3 instead of 5 units of model B, 4 instead of 2 units of model C, and keeping 3 units of model D would increase the gross profit by $26,492.

rate estimates. In addition, the level of standard specifications, selection of materials, construction methods, efficiency of operations, negotiating skills, and scheduling significantly impact cost. Therefore, budgeting adequately for construction cost is not enough: builders, remodelers, and developers must establish and implement standardized processes and procedures to ensure the planned outcome.

Part of the job of a builder, remodeler, or developer is to achieve the projected gross profit margin. This task requires special attention to each construction cost. A well-organized job cost accounting system provides the structure to track construction cost by unit of construction to give managers the information they need to control costs. Chapter 9 presents an overview of job cost accounting.

Establishing a target gross profit ratio (gross profit divided by sales) helps to evaluate whether to accept a contract or build a given plan so use it to weed out jobs or plans that will not meet the desired gross profit ratio. Either reject units or jobs that do not meet the criteria or review them to determine if changes could make the job meet the target.

Also keep in mind that generally builders, remodelers, and developers tend to lose profit margin rather than gain it during construction. In order to achieve profits, you need to plan for profits.

Depending upon a company's operating policies, builders usually can attain a gross profit ratio of 25 to 30%, which allows for a reasonable net profit. Remodeling operations generally require a higher gross profit ratio because of the higher incidence of unknown factors in a remodeling job than in new construction. The same situation is true for land developers. Coupled with the length of time needed to carry out development projects, risk factors demand a higher gross profit ratio—in the 40% range.

## Cash Flow Analysis

The cash flow report is one of the most useful tools available to a builder, remodeler, or developer (fig. 8.3). It identifies sources for and uses of cash within a given period and can serve as a historical statement as well as a planning tool. A historical cash flow report analyzes inflows and outlays of cash in previous periods. Integrate the figures in the cash flow report with those in the balance sheet and income statement for the same period to account for all potential sources and uses of cash.

This cash flow report looks different from the traditional cash flow statement prepared by a CPA as part of standard financial reporting (fig. 8.3). Some builders, remodelers, and developers with small- to medium-sized companies have difficulty understanding the traditional presentation of cash flow. The traditional statement starts with net income, adds back expenses that do not require cash, and then analyzes the balance changes in the balance sheet accounts from the beginning of the period to the end of the period. Those changes will either increase or decrease the cash balance. Although the cash balances in both types of reports may be the same, understanding where cash came from and how it was used is unclear in the traditional statement.

Fortunately, preparing an alternate cash flow report is relatively simple. The report has six major sections as follows:

- beginning cash balance
- receipts (sources of cash)

- disbursements (uses of cash)
- cash requirements
- operating cash loan tracking
- ending cash balance

When preparing cash flow projections, adhere to the guidelines discussed in the following paragraphs.

**Figure 8.3** Cash flow report

| | | |
|---|---:|---:|
| Beginning cash balance | | $ 100,000 |
| Sources of cash | | |
| Sales | $11,330,000 | |
| Collection on receivable | 8,000 | |
| Collection on notes | 14,000 | |
| Deposits by customers | 18,000 | |
| Construction loan draws | 5,954,000 | |
| Total cash receipts | 17,324,000 | |
| Total cash available | | $17,424,000 |
| | | |
| Uses of cash | | |
| Accounts payable | $ 7,973,600 | |
| Payroll, net | 453,200 | |
| Construction loan payments | 8,594,000 | |
| Taxes | | |
| Payroll | 54,900 | |
| Real estate | 9,000 | |
| Deposit on land purchase | 100,000 | |
| Interest | 25,000 | |
| Total disbursements | | $17,209,700 |
| | | |
| Cash balance (A) | | $214,300 |
| Minimum cash-on-hand requirement | | 150,000 |
| Cash excess or shortage | | 64,300 |
| Operating cash loan | | |
| Beginning loan balance | | 250,000 |
| Borrowed funds needed | | |
| Repayment of borrowed funds (B) | | 50,000 |
| Ending loan balance | | $200,000 |
| Ending cash balance (A − B) | | $164,300 |

### Beginning Cash Balance

The cash balance at the end of the previous period becomes the beginning cash balance for the new period.

### Receipts (Sources of Cash)

Analyze all possible cash sources, based on both past experience and on the company's general plan, objectives, and projected level of sales. Identify each source of cash: home sales, remodeling, construction loan draws, land sales, sale of fixed assets, owners' contributions, or other loans. In other words, account for and classify by source all anticipated deposits to the cash account. This analysis requires knowing construction schedules to determine when the company will realize cash. The total of the beginning cash balance and all cash sources for the period constitutes the total cash available.

### Disbursements (Uses of Cash)

The level of activity you have established for your business determines its uses of cash. Look carefully at the sales plan to determine when to repay construction loans. Review the construction schedule to determine payroll needs and approximate pay dates for suppliers and trade contractors. Coordinating with construction schedules is the most challenging step in preparing a cash flow report. Generally, administrative expenses remain the same month after month, regardless of construction, remodeling, or land development activity. However, you must review the annual budget plan for this type of expense and make allowances for expenses that are not paid monthly, such as premiums for vehicles, builder's risk, and Workers' Compensation insurance. Similarly, you should record cash outlays (such as payroll taxes, deposits on estimated income tax, and other expenses not paid monthly) in the period in which they come due.

Financing and marketing expenditures generally relate to the level of sales and construction activities. The timing of these expenses is critical to cash flow.

Examine decisions about the purchase of land, vehicles, and construction or office equipment and incorporate any projected cash outlays in the appropriate budget period.

### Cash Requirements

The company must maintain a minimum cash balance to support its daily business functions. To meet this minimum balance, companies occasionally borrow money from financial institutions in the form of a short-term loan or line of credit. The cash flow report should show the activity of any short-term loans or lines of credit in the cash requirements section.

### Ending Cash Balance

To determine the ending cash balance, deduct cash uses from cash available, and adjust for any operating loan receipts or payments. When preparing a historical cash flow report, ensure that this amount agrees with the ending cash balance on the balance sheet.

Use the historical cash flow report primarily to evaluate a company's past performance and plan for the future. For example, has the company followed plans and objectives? Should you take remedial action if the ending cash balance is not adequate to carry the cash needs for the following period?

The projected cash flow statement analyzes future cash needs, evaluates existing cash resources, and provides timely information about cash needs and cash availability. Accurate cash flow forecasts allow a builder, developer, or remodeler to prearrange lines of credit for periods in which cash flow will be insufficient and/or to explore other potential cash resources before the need for cash becomes critical.

## Financial Ratio Analysis

A ratio is the relationship between two or more numbers. Financial ratios identify relationships among the different classifications in financial statements to measure profitability, financial strength, efficiency of operation, return on investment, and other factors.

Builders, remodelers, and developers find ratios useful as

- planning tools or standards to measure performance
- guidelines to evaluate the position of the business against industry standards
- a means to evaluate historical data and determine trends

Financial ratio analysis helps them to evaluate their individual company's financial position, identify problems to solve and functions or departments to improve, and make decisions that will enhance profitability. Financial ratios measure liquidity, profitability, efficiencies, leverage, and return on investment. Leverage involves using borrowed assets from third parties or resources provided by outsiders to increase the return on an owners' investment.

## Liquidity Ratios

*Liquidity* means solvency or the ability to convert assets to cash. Liquidity ratios evaluate a company's ability to meet short-term cash obligations. Lenders value these ratios because they determine the borrower's ability to repay debt. Monitor the company's liquidity ratio closely to ensure the company can stay in business and maintain its ability to borrow money. Liquidity ratios are explained in more detail in the following sections using figures from the balance sheet shown in figure 7.1.

### Current Ratio
Liquidity or solvency, the ability to pay current debts or liabilities with current assets, is the ratio demonstrated by the following example:

$$\frac{\text{Current assets}}{\text{Current liabilities}} \quad \frac{\$15,685,000}{\$9,200,000} = 1.7$$

Current assets include cash and all other assets that could be converted to cash in the course of normal operations within a fiscal or calendar year (12 months). Current liabilities are debts due to be paid on demand or within a fiscal or calendar year (12 months). The difference between current assets and current liabilities (current assets minus current liabilities) is commonly referred to as working capital:

$$\text{Current assets} - \text{Current liabilities} = \text{Working capital}$$
$$\$15,685,000 \quad - \quad \$9,200,000 \quad = \quad \$6,485,000$$

Working capital consists of resources (current assets) that are available after paying current obligations, and it measures the business's capabilities for expansion and growth.

In this analysis, a high liquidity ratio may be as detrimental as a low ratio because a high ratio of 3 or above indicates inadequate use of available resources. A ratio of 2 is desirable; however, 1.5 is a more typical current ratio in the home building industry.

### Acid Test Ratio

This refinement of the current ratio more strictly tests a company's liquidity. Instead of including all current assets, this ratio uses only "quick assets": cash or any other current asset that can be converted easily to cash within 30 days, such as accounts receivables and short-term cash investments. The acid test ratio does not include inventories. Calculate this ratio as follows:

$$\frac{\text{Quick assets}}{\text{Current liabilities}} = \frac{\$985,000}{\$9,200,000} = 0.11$$

Throughout the industry, and particularly in home building and land development, companies have a low acid test ratio because they are heavily financed and their major current asset is inventory, which does not qualify as quick assets.

## Profitability Ratios

These ratios measure a company's profitability as determined by its revenues. The net income of a business appears in the income statement; therefore, profitability ratios represent relationships among different categories in the income statement as they relate to sales or total revenues. The following examples of profitability ratios use figures from the income statement shown in figure 7.2

**Land Ratio**

$$\frac{\text{Land}}{\text{Sales}} = \frac{\$3,700,000}{\$29,650,000} = 12.5\%$$

**Direct Construction Cost Ratio**

$$\frac{\text{Direct cost}}{\text{Sales}} = \frac{\$17,150,000}{\$29,650,000} = 57.8\%$$

**Cost of Sales Ratio**

$$\frac{\text{Cost of sales}}{\text{Sales}} = \frac{\$20,850,000}{\$29,650,000} = 70.3\%$$

**Gross Profit Ratio**

$$\frac{\text{Gross profit}}{\text{Sales}} = \frac{\$8,800,000}{\$29,650,000} = 29.7\%$$

**Indirect Construction Cost Ratio**

$$\frac{\text{Indirect cost}}{\text{Sales}} = \frac{\$860,000}{\$29,650,000} = 2.9\%$$

**Financing Expense Ratio**

$$\frac{\text{Financing expenses}}{\text{Sales}} = \frac{\$1,560,000}{\$29,650,000} = 5.3\%$$

**Sales and Marketing Expense Ratio**

$$\frac{\text{Sales \& Marketing}}{\text{Sales}} = \frac{\$2,200,000}{\$29,650,000} = 7.4\%$$

**General and Administrative (G&A) Expense Ratio**

$$\frac{\text{General \& Administrative}}{\text{Sales}} = \frac{\$1,425,000}{\$29,650,000} = 4.8\%$$

**Total Operating Expense Ratio**

$$\frac{\text{Total Expenses}}{\text{Sales}} = \frac{\$6,045,000}{\$29,650,000} = 20.4\%$$

**Net Profit Ratio**

$$\frac{\text{Net Profit}}{\text{Sales}} = \frac{\$2,755,000}{\$29,650,000} = 9.3\%$$

Each ratio measures performance for one cost or expense category and shows how that segment of the operation has performed. Establish target ratios for each category and compare actual ratios with target ratios and past periods to determine trends. Pay special attention to the categories that did not hit their targets. Dividing the income statement into these major components helps owners and managers determine where challenges and issues are occurring so they can focus attention on improving functions or departments that are not performing according to plan.

## Efficiency Ratios

To calculate efficiency ratios, use numbers from both the income statement and the balance sheet. They highlight how efficiently the company uses its resources.

The figures used in the following examples are from the balance sheet in figure 7.1 and the income statement in figure 7.2.

### Asset Turnover Ratio
The equation that follows measures how efficiently the company uses its resources (assets) and produces the asset turnover ratio:

$$\frac{\text{Sales}}{\text{Assets}} = \frac{\$29,650,000}{\$17,135,000} = 1.73$$

### Inventory Turnover Ratio

Movement of inventory during a given accounting period is measured by this ratio. Inventories represent a large percentage of a builder's or developer's assets. (A remodeler is generally not as concerned with inventories because a remodeler works under contract without taking ownership of properties.) This ratio allows a builder or developer to evaluate field efficiencies and inventory levels. It reflects construction efficiency and cycle time. The longer the cycle time, the lower the turnover ratio will be. Conversely, the shorter the cycle time is, the higher this ratio will be. Custom builders tend to have a low turnover ratio because their construction cycle is generally long. Developers also will experience a low ratio because of the length of the development process. Excess finished speculative homes affect this ratio unfavorably by lowering it. A higher ratio is better unless the nature of the business dictates a different behavior, as in custom home building and land development. The equation follows:

$$\frac{\text{Sales}}{\text{Inventory}} = \frac{\$29,650,000}{\$14,700,000} = 2.02$$

### Owners' Equity to Total Assets Ratio

The higher this ratio is, the lower the risk to lenders. This ratio shows the percentage of the assets financed by owner investment rather than borrowed funds. The higher this percentage, the lower the risk to the lender as follows:

$$\frac{\text{Owners' equity}}{\text{Assets}} = \frac{\$3,635,000}{\$17,135,000} = 21\%$$

### Ratio of Total Liabilities to Owners' Equity

This ratio is the one most commonly used ratios to measure leverage. The lower the ratio of total liabilities to owners' equity, the stronger the owners' position with respect to the assets of the business as follows:

$$\frac{\text{Liabilities}}{\text{Owners' equity}} = \frac{\$13,500,000}{\$3,635,000} = 3.71$$

Lenders typically look for a ratio of 3 or less; however, this figure varies from region to region, from lender to lender, and by size and structure of a company. With small companies in particular, lenders may work with higher leverage ratios, but they require personal guarantees from the owners to mitigate their risk. For example, lenders may consider the owner's personal assets when evaluating this ratio and may use them as collateral to secure a loan.

Because the ability to borrow money is critical to home builders and developers, be sure to track your company's liquidity and leverage ratios and meet lenders' requirements for making loans. (See "Leverage" later in this chapter.) A company can continue to operate with a loss; however, it cannot operate without cash. Remember, cash is king!

## Return on Investment Ratios

These ratios measure the return on investment with investment defined as either the total resources of a business (total assets) or the owner's investment. The following examples use the numbers from figures 7.1 and 7.2:

**Return on Assets Ratio**

$$\frac{\text{Net profit}}{\text{Assets}} = \frac{\$2,755,000}{\$17,135,000} = 16\%$$

**Return on Owners' Investment Ratio**

$$\frac{\text{Net profit}}{\text{Owners' equity}} = \frac{\$2,755,000}{\$3,635,000} = 76\%$$

The ultimate goal of maximizing profits is to obtain the highest possible return on the owners' investment or capital at risk. With greater risk comes the expectation of higher return. Lower risk usually means smaller returns.

Three ratios impact return on owners' investment. Isolating these ratios helps to determine how to improve the return on investment ratio. *Return on investment* is the product of net profit, efficient use of resources, and degree of leverage.

The following formula expresses the relationships among return on investment, return on sales, asset turnover, and leverage (using credit to improve a business's or owner's financial situation). This formula measures leverage as a relationship of assets to owners' equity instead of debt to owners' equity:

$$\text{Return on investment} = \text{Return on sales} \times \text{Asset turnover} \times \text{Leverage}$$

$$\frac{\text{Profits}}{\text{Equity}} = \frac{\text{Profits}}{\text{Sales}} \times \frac{\text{Sales}}{\text{Assets}} \times \frac{\text{Assets}}{\text{Equity}}$$

$$\frac{\$2,755,000}{\$3,635,000} = \frac{\$2,755,000}{\$29,650,000} \times \frac{\$29,650,000}{\$17,135,000} \times \frac{\$17,135,000}{\$3,635,000}$$

$$76\% = 9.3\% \times 1.73 \times 4.71$$

If you use this formula, the results will be one point higher than when you use the debt-to-owners'-equity formula. An improvement in each of the components will favorably affect return on investment. Exercise caution with the leverage ratio though. A higher leverage ratio indicates a greater return on investment, but also increased risk. Therefore, balance benefits and risks when looking at leverage.

Improving any component of the return on investment formula, or all three, increases the return on invested capital. Planning and control are keys to improving return on invested capital.

## Improving Ratios

The greatest benefit of using ratio analysis is to compare current ratios with those from past periods to determine trends. Looking at the combination of ratios provides a more accurate picture of company performance than analyzing just one or two.

*The Cost of Doing Business Study, 2008 edition*, published by BuilderBooks, explains other ratios prevalent in the industry that are organized by geographical area and sales volume.

### Return on Sales

To make improvements on the return on sales or profits of your company, look at each of the following major components and how they contribute to profit or loss.

### Land Development and Direct Construction Costs

Each home, remodeling job, and lot developed must operate as a cost center with its own account. Within each cost center, break down the costs into subcategories or cost codes using the same codes used in estimating. Then periodically compare actual and estimated costs to make sure actual costs are under control. Pay special attention to variances and change orders.

### Operating Expenses

Financing, sales and marketing, and general and administrative expenses are the three types of operating expenses. These costs are time driven so adhering to schedules is critical to controlling them. Take steps to ensure that your staff and trades follow the plans and balance fixed expenses with sales and production volume. Fixed expenses can become a burden if volume or sales revenues decrease, whereas variable expenses tend to decrease proportionately with volume. A business that minimizes fixed expenses has greater flexibility to withstand the lows of an economic cycle. Standardized systems and procedures help control fixed costs and expenses by increasing the efficiency of the work force.

### Sales Volume

This step requires considerable involvement of the builders, remodelers, or developers and their sales mangers. Two variables impact sales volume: the economic conditions of the marketplace and the company's resources.

Study the marketplace by looking at general economic conditions, local economic conditions, and market trends as well as *NAHB Housing Economics* and forecasts by government agencies and other trade associations.

When analyzing company resources, consider business goals and objectives, services provided, products, available resources, growth potential, additional sources of funds, and management capabilities.

After analyzing economic factors and company resources, develop a meaningful sales plan that accounts for product mix, pricing, and time line. Then manage land, construction materials, and human resource assets to sustain the production level.

### Leverage

The ratio of assets to owners' equity, known as leverage, can be a trade-off, depending on economic conditions. Generally, the trade-off for an increase in leverage is a decrease in return on sales because the increase in borrowing increases interest expenses. An interest-rate increase can dramatically affect a business with high leverage. At the same time, additional capital can generate more sales with the same capital investment by the owners and, thus, potentially increase returns. Use your market knowledge in deciding whether or how much to increase leverage.

### Breakeven Analysis

In essence, *breakeven analysis* attempts to determine the sales volume required to cover all costs and expenses of the company. It can be a quick and easy way to determine minimum sales volume by calculating the number of units, jobs, or lots needed to close in a given period to break even (no profit or loss).

To calculate breakeven, first classify costs and expenses as either variable or fixed costs and expenses. Variable costs and expenses change in direct proportion to increases in volume while fixed costs and expenses stay the same within a volume range. Chapter 3 discusses fixed and variable costs and expenses in detail.

After segregating these costs, calculate the *contribution margin*. It is the difference between sales and variable costs or the margin left to cover fixed expenses as shown in the following example:

Unit sales price – Variable costs and expenses = Contribution margin

To calculate the breakeven point, divide the contribution margin into the fixed cost. The result will be the number of units, jobs, or lots the company needs to sell to reach breakeven (fig. 8.4).

A small adjustment to the formula yields breakeven in dollar volume. This approach is more useful for dealing with a diverse product line; an example follows:

$$\frac{\text{Contribution margin}}{\text{Sales price}} = \frac{\$25,000}{\$100,000} = 0.25$$

Calculate breakeven as follows:

$$\frac{\text{Fixed cost}}{\text{Contribution margin ratio}} = \frac{\$500,000}{0.25} = \$2,000,000$$

The objective of the breakeven analysis is to establish the sales volume needed to cover a company's fixed expenses and when it begins to produce profits. If the sales volume as calculated in the breakeven analysis is not realistic, other options are to improve the contribution margin, reduce fixed costs and expenses, or do both.

Breakeven analysis can determine breakeven for each project or community. Determine the contribution margin or the contribution margin ratio for the project

**Figure 8.4** Calculate the breakeven point

| | |
|---|---|
| Sales price per unit | $ 100,000 |
| Variable costs and expenses per unit | 75,000 |
| Total annual fixed cost | 500,000 |

To calculate the contribution margin:

| | |
|---|---|
| Sales price | $100,000 |
| Variable cost and expenses | 75,000 |
| Contribution margin | $ 25,000 |

To calculate breakeven:

$$\frac{\text{Fixed cost}}{\text{Contribution margin}}$$

$500,000 \div \$25,000$ = 20 units or houses
or 20 units @ $100,000 = $2,000,000

and use only the fixed costs directly related to the project. The result is the number of units or the sales volume the project needs to produce to cover all costs and expenses.

To determine the number of units or sales volume needed to achieve a desirable dollar amount of profits, simply add the desired profit to the fixed cost. If you cannot realistically achieve the established volume with the current level of fixed cost and market conditions one or more factors in the formula will need adjustment.

Builders, remodelers, and developers can also use breakeven analysis as a "what if" analytical tool. They can change any of the numbers in the equation based upon different assumptions to see the impact on profitability. For example, explore the effect of hiring additional staff (which increases fixed cost) on your breakeven point. Or examine the impact of decisions that lower construction cost (variable cost) and increase the contribution margin.

Seeing the potential result of such decisions helps determine whether they are feasible or sensible prior to executing and implementing them. A breakeven analysis allows you to peer into the future.

# CHAPTER 9

# Overview of Job Cost Accounting

The job cost accounting system is a subsystem or subsidiary of the general accounting system that maintains the construction cost detail of each unit under construction. Costs accumulate on a unit-by-unit, job-by-job, or project-by-project basis in the job cost subsidiary. Therefore, the total of all jobs in the job cost subsidiary must equal the total in the direct construction cost account of the general ledger.

The job cost subsidiary provides information for builders, remodelers, and developers to manage, control costs, monitor operations, and make sound business decisions. The list of job cost codes and the integration of the job cost system with estimating, purchasing, and scheduling determines the types and quality of management reports the system can generate.

## Designing the System

The job cost subsidiary has a separate account for each unit of production—a house, a remodeling job, or a parcel of land—in which the construction costs related to that unit accumulate. In addition, each type of cost has its own code for easy tracking.

The cost codes form the basis of the job cost system and create the control points for monitoring construction activity in progress. To maximize the efficiencies of back office systems, each purchasing unit and/or work unit must have its own cost code that represents a pay point. Most importantly, the cost codes in the job cost subsidiary must follow the categories and the order of the cost codes the company uses in estimating and purchasing—usually the construction sequence.

Using the same codes and order facilitates processing and analyzing reports, tightens the field approval process, and helps to maintain adequate control. Coordinating the codes and their order allows easy comparison between estimated cost and actual cost. Code coordination also facilitates easy monitoring and tracking of invoices or requests for payment presented to accounts payable. This comparison of estimated costs to actual costs tracks whether each job performs as expected. The sooner managers know if differences exist between the actual costs and the estimate, the more options the managers have to make correct mistakes and change course on both present and future jobs.

When designing the job cost system, consider the following guidelines because a company's job cost codes must reflect the way it builds, remodels, or develops land, and the nature of its products and services:

- Different geographic areas have different building requirements (such as type of foundation, framing versus block, and the like).

- The use of labor may vary. (Some companies use their own crews, others use trade contractors.)

- Large metropolitan areas might offer a wider range of products and distribution options. (Suppliers and trade contractors might be more or less specialized, depending on their markets.)

- The type of product or service varies from company to company (detached versus attached housing, room additions versus bathroom remodeling, and planned unit developments versus small parcels).

For efficiency, cost codes should follow the construction, remodeling, or development sequence. For this reason, you could close cost code accounts as construction progresses, and thereby, reduce the number of items that a builder, remodeler, or developer must analyze at any particular time. Having the cost codes follow the scheduling sequence helps to integrate invoice approval with scheduling.

To streamline analysis, builders could classify cost codes even further into construction phases. For example, the *preliminary phase* would include all costs incurred prior to the start of construction, such as architectural and engineering fees and permits. The *preparation phase* would include cost codes associated with site clearing, excavation, and foundation. Depending upon construction methods and each company's requirements, builders could have from 3 to 10 construction phases with 5 to 25 cost codes per phase.

For remodelers, the type of remodeling work determines the need for segregating cost codes into phases. For example, phases might not be necessary for a remodeler who mainly does kitchens and baths. However, when remodeling work involves room additions and whole-house remodeling, grouping cost codes by phases might prove helpful. Each phase concentrates attention on a smaller number of cost codes as work progresses.

Developers generally do not require as many cost codes to accumulate development costs as builders need for construction. Therefore, developers may not need to segregate the cost codes into phases, other than to separate the planning phase from the construction phase.

Appendix D presents a sample chart of accounts for job cost codes. When applying the suggested list of cost codes to your business, use only the cost code that represents a purchasing unit or work order. Unnecessary detail hampers the system and produces worthless information that detracts from critical issues. The estimating system is the proper place to maintain the detail behind each job cost code.

For example, when a trade contractor supplies both labor and materials, do not have a cost code for labor and a cost code for material. Having two cost codes creates unnecessary work because you will have to add the dollar amounts in the two cost codes to compare the payment request to the negotiated contract price, which is the control point. However, if you purchase materials from a supplier and the trade agreement includes only labor, you need two cost codes to control the cost of both labor and materials purchased.

If the company issues purchase orders, you should create a cost code for each one. For example, if you order gravel, sand, and concrete block at the same time from the same supplier, you should create only one cost code to accumulate the cost of all three items. However, if you order gravel and sand from a different supplier, you should use two cost codes: one for sand and gravel and one for concrete block. Don't break down an invoice into more than one cost code. Doing so becomes time consuming and increases the chance of entering the cost in the wrong account.

The total dollars spent for each piece of material is irrelevant for accounting purposes. The object is to control the purchasing units estimated prior to the start of construction and that were actually purchased. If invoices do not match estimated amounts, the accountant should catch any discrepancies or variances immediately.

Use the job cost chart of accounts in Appendix D as a guideline or checklist to set up the job cost codes that will meet your needs. A reasonable objective for home builders is to have 75 to 100 cost codes: any more than 100 will begin to clutter the system and hinder the efficient processing of accounting data.

## Job Cost Accounting Review

In summary, in selecting cost codes to use in the job cost accounting system, remember the following guidelines:

- Make it simple. Avoid using more cost codes than you absolutely need.
- Coordinate the job cost codes with your estimating and purchasing functions. One estimating unit must equal one purchasing unit, which in turn represents one pay point or accounts payable unit.
- Follow the construction sequence to facilitate processing and make coordinating electronic field approval of invoices or payment requests easier.
- Make sure the cost codes reflect the way *you* build.
- Have a cost code for the special things you sometimes include in your homes, even if you do not add them to all of your homes, such as special flooring or finishes. You will have the cost code set up when you do need to use it.
- Break down cost codes into material and labor only if you supply the material and subcontract just for the labor. Otherwise, use one cost code to keep track of the total contract. If your trades receive multiple payments, create a separate cost code for each one. Tie the payments to specific stages of completion rather than the percentage of completion. Spell out payment requirements in your trade contractor agreements.
- Prepare accurate estimates for each house you build.
- Compare invoices to your estimates to ensure that you pay what you agreed to and don't pay too much.
- Review each home built by comparing the estimate to the actual cost. This analysis will help determine where profits are leaking and direct you to the problems. It will also enhance estimating skills because it will identify cost codes where estimates were not done correctly.

## Coding Invoices

Accurate coding of invoices is essential to any job cost accounting system. Cost reports are useless unless the data presented is accurate and reliable. The coding of invoices is generally the weak link in a job cost accounting system. By the time your company receives the invoices, employees may not remember why the materials were purchased or where they were used. Answering these questions becomes a guessing game. Moreover, occasionally invoices get lost, misplaced, or damaged while they are being coded.

Establish a system that will facilitate the coding process and ensure reliable reports. A purchase order system provides the best solution to the coding challenge because the person ordering materials or scheduling labor codes the purchase orders when ordering materials or scheduling labor. However, if a purchase order system is not in place, use the cost code number as the purchase order number when you order materials from suppliers. The cost code will then appear on the invoice as the purchase order number. Keep in mind that invoices also need to reference the job for which the materials were delivered or the work done. Therefore, place a separate order for each individual job: suppliers and trades are reasonably accurate when they are identifying the location to which deliveries were made or where work was done.

## Improving Control with a Purchase Order System

A purchase order system provides many advantages, including the following:

- confirms a verbal or telephone purchase
- confirms anticipated delivery dates
- fixes the price on will-call orders
- provides written records of purchases
- gives the superintendent a reference or control point to check quantity and quality of materials delivered
- serves as proof of delivery and authorization for payment
- facilitates job cost posting and accounting
- allows a builder, remodeler, or developer to delegate much of the purchasing function to non-managers
- provides a reference to quoted prices
- gives current information on outstanding obligations
- protects the trades' lien rights (The trades need to clearly identify where they have done the work to be able to exercise their lien rights. The purchase order system clearly identifies the location of the work and amounts owed to the trade for that work.)

## Preparing Job Cost Reports

Reports generated by the job cost system must be timely and standardized, and they must include the following information for each unit or remodeling job under construction or for each project being developed:

- budget and actual costs
- variances or differences between budget and actual costs
- committed cost or outstanding purchase orders

The overall objective of a job cost control system is to produce accurate cost information that builders, remodelers, and developers can use to increase the profitability of their businesses. Therefore, make sure each cost code represents a point of control. The job cost reports should highlight variances.

With a well-functioning estimating and purchasing system and a reliable cost accounting system, a company can focus on controlling variances. Many accounting software systems facilitate tracking variances by reason, community, superintendent, and home so you can eradicate the variances and prevent reoccurrences.

# CHAPTER 10

# Processing Systems

**A**ccounting involves processing large quantities of data so you can prepare financial and management reports necessary for the operation and management of a business.

## Computing Options

Owning a computer is now a necessity for even the smallest-volume builder, remodeler, or developer. Computers are affordable, and the software choices for home building, remodeling, and land development businesses have increased.

Although a manual accounting system can work effectively and produce high-quality reports, it is labor intensive, time consuming, and prone to human error. Purchasing a computer should be considered a cost of doing business.

Many builders, remodelers, and developers believe the best processing system is an in-house computer system because it expedites data entry, and they can generate reports whenever they need them. A number of accounting packages designed for the non-accountant take care of much of the accounting processing behind the screen. They also make the data entry quite friendly to almost every user.

If you still use an outside service, at the bare minimum, work with the outside accountant and provide him or her with a list of the reports and information you need.

The integrity of the information and the usefulness of the reports that come from the accounting system depend upon the accuracy of data entry and the accounts you use to classify the data. Follow the NAHB Chart of Accounts (Appendix B) to obtain the best possible output from your accounting system.

## Computerizing the Accounting Function

When computerizing their accounting functions, builders, remodelers, and developers should beware the myth that computers solve all the problems of processing accounting data and that they provide timely and accurate reports. The old axiom, "Garbage in, garbage out," still holds true.

A computerized accounting system requires efficient and disciplined financial procedures and a reporting system, including procedures for entering, processing, storing (or filing) information and updating files. Protect your files and computer software by using passwords and backups. (Remember to change passwords regularly.) Well-documented procedures and controls, with clearly identified reporting requirements, are essential for the smooth operation of a computerized accounting system.

When builders, remodelers, or developers implement new software or change to a new system, they should allow extra time to learn the new system. Some systems are easier to implement than others, and they may have a shorter learning curve, but remember that people learn at different speeds. Implementing any new system often takes strong perseverance. Many failures occur at this stage because a builder, remodeler, or developer lacks the commitment and decisiveness necessary to ensure implementation. After implementation, daily operations will improve, especially with small systems.

## Accounting Applications

Builders, remodelers, and developers benefit from an integrated accounting system that posts the data to the general and subsidiary ledgers and also interacts with management reporting functions. Even if you start by computerizing only the accounting function, choose software that eventually can integrate other business functions, including sales, budgeting, estimating, purchasing, scheduling, cost control, warranty, and other record-intensive activities.

When you are shopping for a computer, purchase hardware that meets the following criteria:

- Meets your current needs and can be upgraded to meet changing needs
- Is compatible with the accounting software packages you need and with other software applications you anticipate needing
- Is as powerful as you can afford
- Includes a strong support package from the vendor or a third party for the crucial installation phase, including a toll-free number for troubleshooting via telephone during the life of the hardware (When you request their advice, service representatives should be able to make recommendations for enhancements and improvements to the system)
- Provides reliable and outstanding support service from the vendor or a third party because computer down time can prove extremely costly
- Has enough disk storage to run your software efficiently

To be certain you purchase a computer system that will match your needs, attend NAHB-sponsored seminars and workshops on computer software at the International Builders' Show (IBS) and other professional meetings. If necessary, seek the advice of a professional computer consultant.

When shopping for software, look for user-friendly, integrated accounting and cost control packages that meet your requirements and reporting needs. As you research software packages, ask vendors how long they have been in business and how many users are presently on the system. Ask for a list of builder, remodeler, or developer references at companies that are similar in size to yours, do similar work, have purchased the package, and can offer an opinion. Call several of the references and, if possible, visit the user's office that most closely resembles your operation. Ask questions about their experience and discuss whether the software has met their expectations. Ask about implementation and find out what was easy and what was difficult. This information will help you evaluate the software.

## Storage

An automated accounting system stores data in a database that builders, remodelers, and developers can house either locally or remotely. One software package, with one database running on one computer, is the simplest example of a local database. It is designed for one user to access the information at a time.

Builders, remodelers, and developers also may store data locally on a server (sometimes referred to as a file or database server). A server connects two or more computers by using a hub that allows more than one user to access the same information. Server-based software offers the following advantages:

- ready access to the information by multiple users

- faster performance of the system

- ease of maintenance of the software (Much of the maintenance can be done on the server)

- ease of backing up data (The server backs up data automatically)

How you structure your organization helps determine whether you need remote access to company data. Builders, remodelers, and developers cite being able to access data wherever they need to or want to as their primary reason for obtaining remote access. Historically, the *wide area network* or WAN) that allowed remote access typically required a higher level of technical staffing at both the central and remote locations.

The Internet now gives small-volume builders, remodelers, and developers the same capabilities as a wide area network. Software systems that run on the Internet (sometimes called *Application Service Providers* (ASPs) or Web-based systems) require only that builders, remodelers, or developers have a high-speed connection, such as DSL or a cable modem.

An ASP system reduces the builder's, remodeler's, or developer's investment in hardware, software maintenance, and technical staff while the company benefits from having access to its data from any authorized Internet connection. With such a system, information is available around the clock without the special requirements of a WAN system. Because large- and small-volume builders alike benefit from Internet-ready software, stay abreast of new developments and changes in hardware and software, which change constantly.

Making the Internet an integral part of software applications and programs is becoming more commonplace. Although using the Internet can save time and money, business owners must ensure that they protect their systems and data with a secure site or a firewall because the Internet can present an open door to hackers. Therefore, if you are unsure of the security of your software or data, ask for help from a trusted professional.

## Other Applications

Computer versatility and software availability allow builders, remodelers, and developers to explore many practical and efficient computer applications. Popular programs, other than accounting, can be grouped into four primary categories as follows:

1. Word processing and desktop publishing programs
2. Spreadsheets or electronic worksheets
3. Database management programs
4. Drawing and computer-aided design (CAD) programs

Each type has numerous versions available, each with different features and levels of sophistication. Technology advancements in Windows® and Internet browsers have made these programs more user friendly.

Word processing systems save time and enhance the professional quality of such documents as form letters, contract formats, and standard notices.

Spreadsheets are great analytical and planning tools. With them builders, remodelers, and developers can prepare management reports easily because these programs accurately perform mathematical functions and allow quick recalculation of projected outcomes based on various scenarios. Database management programs store and sort statistical information; maintain mailing lists; collect and analyze sales and production data; track personnel, clients, and prospects; and perform other functions.

*CAD programs* are increasingly popular among building, remodeling, and development firms. These programs can serve as sales tools because they allow clients to view the results of architectural changes on a computer screen. Builders or remodelers using CAD can alter plans quickly and at minimal cost, and developers can use CAD to create site plans. Many CAD programs also can produce "intelligent plans" that integrate material selections into the plans and provide takeoffs.

Today, computer technology is continually changing. Therefore, you or an objective computer professional must stay abreast of new hardware and software developments. For example, recent World Wide Web–based applications increase connectivity to suppliers, trades, prospects, and home owners.

In addition, more builders, remodelers, and developers are utilizing Web-based technology to streamline their paper trails and communications. The Internet continues its rapid expansion, and it can significantly change the way you do business if it hasn't already done so. Understanding how prospects, buyers, trades, vendors, and others use the Internet, helps you use it to reach them more effectively and helps potential customers reach you.

Computers are affordable tools that are no longer optional. They are crucial to the effective management of a building, remodeling, or land development firm. If you do not use a computer now, consider beginning to do research and educate yourself to incorporate computers into your daily operations. If you are already using a computer and not taking full advantage of its capabilities, begin keeping abreast of upgrades and new developments that will make your computer easier to use and further enhance your business.

# CHAPTER 11

# Tips for Multiple-Project Companies

**W**hen companies work on more than one project or community simultaneously, each project operates like a miniature company within the main company. Therefore, this chapter defines the term *project* in a broader sense than one specific job. In this context, *project* refers to land parcels or communities with multiple sites or to specific groups of like activities (such as remodeling projects, light commercial projects, framing, or other miscellaneous activities).

Builders, remodelers, and developers should identify the contribution each project makes to the overall profitability of their companies and evaluate each project on its merit.

A key factor in increasing profitability is to identify problems promptly. Measuring the performance of a multiple-project firm on a project-by-project or community-by-community basis helps isolate problems. In addition, builders should further evaluate performance by model or floor plan, remodelers by the type of job, and developers by the type of lot. This chapter focuses primarily on the project level.

When a company diversifies into more than one activity (such as home building and development, remodeling and custom building, or any combination of activities), it should treat each activity as a separate project and profit center. Therefore, account for each project with subprojects or communities within each activity if required. Some companies also employ their own trades; for example, framers, finish carpenters, and drywall installers. Each of the activities needs to be treated as a separate profit center and managed as a trade company to ensure adequate performance. Measure the productivity of each crew to ensure that the cost of running the crew is competitive in the marketplace.

## General Accounting

A multiple-project company uses the same accounting structure as a single-project company. Sales for each project or community must be recorded at the community level along with costs and expenses directly associated with the community. Most accounting software can record the activity for each community or project and aggregate the projects to report the activity of the company as a whole. Some software programs refer to this capability as tracking revenues and expenses by division or departments.

When builders have different types of housing units in a subdivision, such as single-family-detached homes, patio homes, and townhomes), they should set up separate revenue and cost of sales accounts to track the different product lines.

## Chart of Accounts

The NAHB Chart of Accounts is designed to expand with a company's growth. As a single-project company grows into a multiple-project company it may need additional accounts. For example, because the owner or top manager of a small company usually has direct control of all communication devices, that small company can use a single account for all communications expenses. However, as the company grows and adds new employees, it will use more mobile phones and radios. To exercise better control over these expenditures, the company should set up separate expense accounts for office phones, mobile phones, and radios.

A need for increased control triggers expansion of the chart of accounts rather than taking on multiple projects. As the company grows, owners and top managers tend move further away from day-to-day operations, and they need additional accounts to control expenses.

Each project or subdivision must use the same structure or chart of accounts to accumulate sales revenue and cost of sales. Many software programs allow the bookkeeper to record and report financial data by department, division, or project. As the bookkeeper enters revenues and expenses, the software (if it is loaded properly) will ask for the department, division, or project number. Then it will automatically store the information by those three categories.

Evaluate each project on its own merit because each one must contribute to the overall profitability of the company. Analysis of contribution margin (sales minus lot cost, direct construction cost, and direct community expenses) and gross profit margin (sales minus lot cost and direct construction cost) is paramount at the project level (see Chapter 8 for details).

The accounting system should be able to identify problems such as low sales volume or high direct construction costs as they occur or soon after. You can measure the profitability of each project by accumulating revenues by project and matching the cost of sales and expenses directly to project revenues.

## Profit Centers

Establishing each project as a separate profit center is the first step in maximizing profitability. Classifying revenues, cost of sales, and direct project expenses on a project-by-project basis creates profit centers that owners and managers can track and analyze. Each project has a separate budget with a projected contribution margin so they can compare actual results to planned performance. This comparison helps owners and managers evaluate each project and identify cost control problems more easily.

In addition, the profitability of each project will provide a measurement of management performance. Depending upon the size of the organization and the number and size of the projects, one manager could be responsible for more than one project.

## Contribution Margin

The critical profitability measurement for a project or community is the contribution margin or *operating profit*. It represents the income generated by the project or its contribution to the general overhead and profit of the company. The contribution margin of a community includes the income, cost, and expenses that relate only to that specific community. It contributes to the overall profit of the company; therefore, it sometimes is referred to as operating profit. Lack of a contribution margin or a negative contribution margin indicates that the company lost money in operating the project and that the project consumed resources from other projects.

Cost and expenses above the contribution margin would not be incurred if the project did not exist. Typical direct cost and expenses to the projects are as follows:

- lot costs
- direct construction costs
- supervision and field salaries for staff assigned to the project
- construction office facilities and related on-site expenses
- interest and other finance expenses related to the construction and sale of houses in the project
- cost of the model home complex
- on-site sales office expenses
- internal and outside commissions paid on the sale of the houses
- advertising and promotional expenses that relate exclusively to the project

To calculate the contribution margin, deduct from the sales of the projects the costs and expenses that are direct to the project.

The contribution margin does not include expenses that apply to the entire company. These expenses include, but are not limited to, the following:

- salaries for the administrative team and accounting department
- marketing expenses such as development of logos, stationery, and institutional ads
- financing expenses applicable to the financing of office equipment and other assets

Creating profit centers for all projects and special activities and calculating the contribution margin for each project, helps identify profit leaks. In some cases, making changes can turn projects around. In other cases, liquidating or selling the project to a competitor may be the best solution.

## Job Costing

Job costing works the same for a multiple-project company, as for a single-project company with one exception. You should still estimate job costs on a house-per-house basis and accumulate actual costs in 1430, direct construction cost, and the job cost subsidiary. Then follow the same procedures and use the same reports to control the costs as outlined in Chapter 9.

However, the numbering system used to identify units of construction may need adjustment. Simply add project numbers to each unit number. For example, if you use block and lot numbers to identify each unit of production, the house under construction on block 4, lot 23, in project 12 would be known as unit 120423. The first two digits identify the project; the second two digits, the block; and the last two digits, the lot. You could also use letters instead of numbers to identify projects. The numbering system should clearly identify projects and allow grouping of cost reports by project for managers responsible for each project.

## Indirect Construction Cost

As discussed in Chapter 2, indirect construction costs are necessary for construction, but not directly connected with a particular unit. Some examples of indirect construction cost include supervisory cost, cost of field vehicles, temporary utilities, and construction offices.

Although indirect costs are not directly tied to a production unit, they are direct costs for a project and, as such, should be accounted for as part of the project. The project manager is responsible for controlling these costs. Allocating indirect construction costs to each project helps owners ascertain the profitability of a particular project, as well as evaluate the project manager's performance.

If estimating, purchasing, and design functions are performed in a central location, these costs are indirect to the project and are a cost to the company, not the project. To allocate the total indirect cost for each project to the units built in each project, follow any of the methods described in Chapter 7.

## Sales, Marketing, and Financing Expenses

Distribute the sales, marketing, and financing expenses directly related to a particular project to that project. The company would not have incurred these expenses if the project did not exist.

## General and Administrative Expenses

Normally, you cannot charge general and administrative expenses directly to individual projects because they relate to the company as a whole. Avoid trying to allocate expenses that are shared by multiple projects, such as administrative and accounting salaries, marketing expenses that benefit more than one project, and other such types of expenditures. Because project managers have little or no control over these expenditures, allocating these expenses to projects generally does not provide useful information for managing projects or evaluating their efficiency.

## Financial Analysis

To accomplish a financial analysis of a multiple-project company, take the following steps (see Chapter 8 for details):

1. Prepare income statements (profit and loss statements) for each project. The net result for each project is its contribution margin.
2. Divide the contribution margin by the sales price to determine the contribution margin ratio.
3. Divide gross profit by sales to calculate the gross profit ratio.
4. Make comparisons between projects, time periods, and projected results.
5. Establish trends for projects by comparing previous to present ratios.

If projects are set up as separate companies and accountability extends to a group of investors, allocate company-wide expenses to each project only after determining the contribution margin. This practice helps to maintain a clear picture of project performance.

In addition to income statements by project, prepare and analyze an income statement that includes all of the company's revenue-generating activities and analyze it following the guidelines in Chapter 8.

# CHAPTER 12

# Tips for Developers

Some members of the light construction industry only develop land; some single-family builders diversify into land development as their companies grow. Although many similarities exist between home building and land development, some factors pertain only to land development, and they merit consideration.

- Because of financing equity requirements, the initial capital investment required for land development is generally larger and of longer duration than the capital investment required for home building.

- Because of this long time frame—from the initial land acquisition and negotiation phase through the approval process and completion of the development project—the risk factor is usually higher than for home building.

- Land development projects are subject to lengthy approval processes requiring numerous local, state, and federal government approvals.

- Home owners in neighboring subdivisions could have an impact on the design and specifications of the land plan.

- The technical nature of the planning and design requires the involvement of highly-trained engineers, land planners, and specialists in sensitive environmental issues.

- Two elements of the successful completion of a land development project are market analysis and feasibility studies.

## General Accounting

The principles of general accounting, internal control, and financial analysis presented in this publication are applicable to land development companies, as well as to building companies that diversify into other construction activities, including land development. When performing more than one economic activity (home building, remodeling, and/or land development), account for each activity in a separate profit center to accurately evaluate the performance of each.

Beyond accounting for these activities separately, the processes and procedures of recording the accounting information do not change. The NAHB Chart of Accounts presented in Appendix A sets up the structure to allow for the separate accountability of land development activities. The general accounting procedures for a developer vary little from those of a home builder.

Recognition of revenues for a land development operation follows the same guidelines as recognition of income for a home building business. Land development businesses recognize revenues at the time the title of the land transfers from the land development company to a bona fide purchaser. The purchaser can be an unrelated party or a subsidiary company that will build homes on the finished lots.

For internal control, developers (or builders diversifying into development) must follow the same rules to separate duties, properly account for funds, and follow standard practices and procedures as presented in Chapter 6. Guidelines for cash management presented in Chapter 8 are universal as well and, therefore, apply to land development companies. Developers also must coordinate their accounting systems with their estimating and purchasing systems. The timeline from land acquisition to completion of land improvements for each development project is particularly critical for optimizing project success.

A land development company's financial statements follow the same format as for a home building company; and the accountant would analyze them similarly but would use lots or parcels instead of housing units. Chapter 8 discusses a number of financial ratios for gauging a company's performance. These ratios are the same for builders, remodelers, and developers. However, if a company is involved in both land development and home building, the owner must account for each activity independently of the others then measure the profitability of each activity. In other words, treat the land development operations of a home building company (or the building operations of a land development company) as a separate profit center.

Account for land development revenues, costs, and expenses as if the development operation was an independent company that transfers finished lots to the building operation or building company at market value rather than at cost. By making the land development activities a separate profit center, builders and developers can evaluate the profitability of each activity and clearly identify whether problems uncovered in the profit equation result from land development or home building.

## Chart of Accounts

The NAHB Chart of Accounts presented in Appendix A is suitable for a land development company. Asset account 1410, land and land development costs, accumulates (1) the acquisition costs of undeveloped tracts of land and (2) the development costs to convert the tracts of land into developed or finished lots. On the liability side, 2220, acquisitions and development loans payable, records the development and construction loans payable. Use 2230, construction loans payable, to record the construction loans.

The revenue and cost of sales section of the NAHB Chart of Accounts has separate accounts for recording the sales and cost of sales of undeveloped tracts of land. You also should allocate sales of developed lots and the lot costs to a separate revenue account. Recording revenue and cost of sales of different activities in separate accounts allows you to measure each activity separately and evaluate its contribution to the company's overall profitability.

## Job Costing

Account 1410, land and land development, accumulates all costs relating to acquisition and development of raw land. This account offers no details about the types of costs or the parcel of land to which they relate. As with control of direct construction costs in the home building operation, control of these costs in land development is critical to achieving maximum profit. Thus, the developer needs a subsidiary system, similar to the job cost system working behind 1430. Appendix F presents a list of the accounts iu the land development job cost subsidiary.

As with home building costs, the developer also needs to keep the costs for each parcel of land or each development project separate from the others. Separating costs by development project allows the developer to evaluate each project individually and simultaneously establish the cost base for distributing the development costs to the finished lots in each project. Because land parcels differ, site costs could vary significantly depending on site conditions (for example, wooded versus cleared). Chapter 9 describes the use of the job cost subsidiary of account 1430. The job cost subsidiary of 1410, land and land development, functions the same way.

## Development Cost

Developers normally divide a development project into multiple phases. As lots sell, developers open additional phases. Each phase needs a separate budget. Collect the actual costs by phase as well to compare with the budget and ensure that development costs stay within it.

Developing the first phase of a project may cost more than developing additional phases. This difference occurs because local jurisdictions often collect fees and exactions (such as impact fees, recreation fees, contributed acreage) for an entire development during the first phase of a multiphase project. In addition, entrance signs, initial utility runs to the site, amenities and common-area landscaping often add to the costs at the start of a project. However, all completed lots must share a portion of the start-up, common-area, and amenities costs. Therefore, developers need to base cost allocations on the projected total cost of the project. Accurate planning and estimating help control actual costs so they don't get out of control toward the end of a project and result in the last lots absorbing cost overruns.

When developing more than one subdivision simultaneously, a developer must treat each one as a separate profit center. The accounting guidelines are similar to those for home builders with multiple projects. Chapter 11 includes a detailed discussion about how to handle cost control and accounting procedures with more than one project in process.

## Indirect Costs

The necessary production costs that are not directly associated with the finished product are indirect costs. Examples of indirect costs include supervision, construction trailers, field office expenses, and temporary utilities. Direct costs include water and sewer pipe, curbs and gutters, pools and other amenities included in the land development plans. Such costs may be indirect to the lots, but direct to the project. Therefore, you must add them to the development cost to determine the total cost to allocate to the developed lots.

## Financing Costs

Financing costs for development projects are considered part of the cost of the project. As such, developers cannot write them off in the period in which they are incurred. Instead, they become part of the total cost of the project, and developers would allocate them to each individual lot.

## Lot Cost Allocation

Because of the length of the development process and the practice of doing development work in phases, lot-cost allocation troubles some developers. However, these developers have other options.

For a track of land developed all at once, divide the total cost of acquisition and development by the number of finished or developed lots. This method works under the assumption that the cost to develop each lot in the tract is the same. Of course, the profit margin for a higher-priced lot (wooded, lake front, views) would be higher than the profit margin for the less desirable or lower-priced lots. Some developers believe the higher-priced lots should carry a higher percentage of the cost because often building on these lots is more expensive: for instance, the houses may have walk-out basements.

Developers who follow this school of thought take a market approach to lot-cost allocation: They determine the percentage of the total market value that is represented by the market value of each lot. For example, imagine a small parcel developed into five lots. The market value of each lot and the percentage of the total market value represented by each lot would be as follows:

| Lot no. | Market value | Percentage of total |
|---------|--------------|---------------------|
| 1 | $65,000 | 21% |
| 2 | 68,000 | 24 |
| 3 | 61,000 | 19 |
| 4 | 58,000 | 15 |
| 5 | 65,000 | 21 |

The developer would divide the total cost of the land development ($120,000) among the lots, based on the percentage of the development's total market value that the market value of each lot represents. An example follows:

| Lot No. | Calculation | Development cost |
|---------|-------------|------------------|
| 1 | .21 × $120,000 | $25,200 |
| 2 | .24 × 120,000 | 28,800 |
| 3 | .19 × 120,000 | 22,800 |
| 4 | .15 × 120,000 | 18,000 |
| 5 | .21 × 120,000 | 25,200 |
| | | $120,000 |

When developers use this method, each lot shows the same gross profit ratio because the costs are distributed to each lot in proportion to its value. (See Chapter 8 for a discussion of gross profit.)

In a multiphase development, the initial phase or phases include costs that all lots in the project must share. Examples include costs associated with the zoning process, heavy front-end utility installations, off-site improvements required by local jurisdictions, and amenities. You can allocate these costs to the developed lots in one of two ways: you can complete phases and put lots on the market as follows:

1. Divide the total estimated development by the total number of lots to be developed to determine the unit cost or use the market-approach method described above. Periodically, revise the total estimated development cost to include variances incurred in all phases, including the most recent phase, and change the allocation to each lot from that point forward to reflect changes or discrepancies with the earlier estimate.

2. Isolate the common-area costs from the other costs of each phase. To use this method, allocate to each lot a portion of the common costs and a portion of the development costs for the phase. Developers may want to use this method if (1) great variations in the layout of the land would cause significant variations in development costs per phase or (2) the phases have significant market value variations. Chapter 15 discusses in more detail various acceptable options for allocating acquisition and development costs to individual lots.

## Lot Pricing

Market forces influence lot pricing whether the developer sells the lots to an unrelated party or puts them into production. Yet some builders distort their profit margins from home building because they use a lower-than-market-cost basis for developed lots. Owners and top managers need to evaluate the profitability of each segment or activity of the company independently. Therefore, profit margins for the home building operations should not include development profits.

## Financial Analysis

Developers also can use the tools, test, and ratios discussed in Chapter 8 along with the material in this chapter to evaluate the financial performance of a development company or operation.

# CHAPTER 13

# Tips for Remodelers

emodelers typically function as general contractors and do not carry inventories or construction financing during the building process. They are under
contract to improve a customer's property, with the customer usually financing the construction cost. As a general contractor, the remodeler sometimes has to
post a performance bond for the amount of the remodeling contract while home
builders typically do not have to post such bonds.

Many single-family builders diversify into remodeling when economic slumps
cause potential move-up buyers to remodel their existing homes instead of buying
new ones. Some companies work exclusively in remodeling, and others, whose
main operation is remodeling, diversify into new single-family construction, usually custom homes.

No matter what combination of activities a company performs, anyone who
makes remodeling a part of his or her business must recognize that remodeling is a
different type of operation from new construction, and it requires separate accountability. Builders who diversify into different construction activities, such as
remodeling, must identify and account for each activity separately.

## General Accounting

This chapter applies the principles of general accounting, internal control, and financial analysis specifically to a remodeling company. Although the processes and
procedures of recording financial information do not change, the NAHB Chart of
Accounts (Appendix D) sets up the structure to account for remodeling activities
separately from home building or development activities.

Recognizing remodeling income can differ from recognizing new construction
income. The nature and size of the remodeling jobs and the size of the company
typically influence how to recognize remodeling income. Usually a remodeler
works under contract and, therefore, does not need a work-in-progress inventory
account. The company recognizes revenue as it bills the job, and it recognizes cost
of sales as it receives invoices. However, remodelers still must maintain control

over remodeling costs by comparing estimated and actual costs and preparing a variance analysis report on each job. Accounting for and controlling costs ensures superior profit. If your company buys houses to fix up and resell, you should account for that activity as a separate profit center.

Guidelines for internal control, as presented in Chapter 6, apply to remodeling operations as well. They include separating crucial financial duties, properly accounting for funds, and standardizing practices and procedures. Cash management guidelines are universal, as is the need to coordinate job cost accounting with estimating and purchasing.

A remodeling company should follow the same format for financial statements and financial analysis as for a home building company. Chapter 8 discusses a number of financial ratios that help a builder, remodeler, or developer evaluate a company's performance. Even though a remodeling company uses the same ratio analysis, target ratios will be different for a /remodeling operation than for a home building company. For example, because of the risk involved in the unknown aspects of many remodeling jobs, the gross profit ratio for remodeling should be significantly higher than for new construction:

$$\text{Gross profit ratio} = \frac{\text{Gross profit}}{\text{Sales}}$$

In this ratio, gross profit equals sales, minus cost of sales. A sensible target for a gross profit ratio for new construction is generally 25 to 30%. Remodelers should aim for a ratio of 35 to 45%, depending upon the nature of the remodeling operations and typical unknown factors.

Marketing and financing expenses for remodeling are considerably less than for new construction because generally in remodeling the owner or client secures project financing. Remodelers who pay sales commissions would allocate them to sales and marketing expenses.

Remodeling requires closer supervision of the work to ensure customer satisfaction. Therefore, a remodeling company generally will have higher supervisory and administrative costs than a new construction company. An accountant would treat indirect construction costs for a remodeling operation as period expenses because remodeling jobs require no inventories. Therefore, remodelers do not need to allocate indirect costs to jobs. Because most indirect construction costs are fixed (remain unchanged regardless of volume), remodelers must control them.

Remodelers tend to use less trade contract labor and more payroll labor than builders. Using company employees to do the work can provide better quality control. However, having employees increases fixed costs and escalates the need to coordinate expenses with volume. Company employees also may require more supervision to ensure adequate productivity.

In remodeling, the target for net profit before taxes should be 10 to 15%, the same as for new construction. Sound management practices and proper accountability are vital to both builders and remodelers. However, the interplay of factors that contribute to or detract from profitability varies between new construction and remodeling. Therefore, account for remodeling activities separately from other activities to correctly evaluate the remodeling operation's performance.

## Chart of Accounts

The chart of accounts for a remodeling operation should be the same as the chart presented in Appendix A. The balance sheet accounts, assets, liability, and owners' equity all apply to a remodeling operation. However, expand the income statement accounts, revenues, cost of sales, and expenses to create separate accounts for accumulating the accounting data from remodeling activities. Appendix D lists the recommended accounts and account numbers to accumulate the revenues, cost of sales, and expenses of remodeling.

Refer to Chapter 11 for guidelines on how to account for the remodeling operation as a separate project.

## Credit Approval

Unlike new construction, in most cases remodeling is financed by the owner without a financial institution or lender supervising the release of funds. Therefore, remodelers set up a credit approval procedure to ensure full payment upon job completion.

Depending on a job's size and dollar volume, remodelers can take several avenues to perform credit checks on potential clients. Membership in a credit-rating company provides a sound option for checking credit worthiness. Also, obtain and follow up on credit references from the client.

On large jobs not financed by a lender, set up a joint account that contains funds for the total amount of the contract and stipulate that the release of funds requires the signatures of both the owner and the remodeler. The use of reputable escrow agents is another option for large jobs. In addition, contracts must include specific terms and conditions for securing final payment. Many remodelers' contracts specify use of arbitration in the event of a dispute.

Monitor change orders closely and resist the temptation to perform work outside the scope of the original contract or subsequent change orders. If you do decide to perform additional work, have the client sign a change order covering the work and collect payment for such work in advance. Furthermore, make sure the client is aware of the impact of those changes on the total cost of the job and take precautions to avoid financial surprises upon completion.

## Job Costing

The profitability of a remodeling operation rests on controlling construction costs so the principles for home builders, discussed in Chapter 9, also apply to remodelers. Alternatively, you can account for the costs of remodeling by accumulating remodeling costs in account 1430, direct construction cost, instead of recording them as cost of sales in the 3800 series of accounts, costs of construction—remodeling.

The job cost subsidiary will accumulate the costs on a job-by-job basis, using job cost accounts as points of control during the remodeling process. Use the same job cost accounts to estimate jobs and record costs. This coordination will facilitate variance analysis. Assign a number to each job to identify it in the subsidiary account—the foundation of the control system, Require invoices to show the job number and the cost code provided to the supplier, trade contractor, or other vendor when your company placed the order. Proper coding of invoices ensures the reliability of data collected in the job cost subsidiary. Refer to Chapter 9 for a detailed discussion of job costing concepts.

## Completed Contracts

A small remodeling company that maintains its accounting records on a cash basis records revenues from remodeling operations when it collects the revenue, and it records the costs and expenses when it pays for them. Because remodelers do not create inventories, this method of recognizing income, costs, and expenses is acceptable; and it simplifies accounting. However, for control purposes, the cash method delays the processing of key financial information.

To obtain more timely financial information, use the accrual method of accounting. If you also use the completed-contract method, you are better able to match revenues with costs. When you use the completed-contract method of revenue recognition, you postpone the recognition of income and costs until the job is done. During the remodeling process, accumulate costs in account 1430, and transfer them to cost of sales when you complete the work. You would accumulate payments collected during the remodeling process in 2010, contract deposits, and transfer them to the revenue account when you complete the work. This method provides a more accurate measure of profit because it matches revenues and costs to the completed jobs.

# CHAPTER 14

# Financial Planning and Budget

## Structure

The financial plan or budget provides direction and improves the coordination and control of a building, remodeling, or land development business. Base your budgets on thorough research and data analysis that takes into account internal resources and general economic trends and opportunities.

The owner and top management team are responsible for the company's budget process. However, to ensure that employees will accept and carry out the budget, they should help prepare the portion of it for which they are responsible and will be held accountable. Typically, accounting coordinates the effort and compiles the numbers in the final document.

Financial planning provides the following advantages:

- formally establishes the company's objectives and direction
- enables the company to use available resources more efficiently and effectively
- helps coordinate and control staff responsibilities within the firm
- directs capital toward the most profitable channels
- helps control specific operations and expenditures
- serves as a communication device within the organization
- establishes a standard against which a builder, remodeler, or developer can evaluate company performance

For the budgeting process to succeed, the building, remodeling, or development firm should meet the following requirements:

- Prepare the budget or financial plan prior to the period it will cover. For a one-year plan, start at least two months before the beginning of the period and set budgets for each month of the year. For example, if your company operates on a calendar year, begin planning in early November.
- Define lines of authority as well as each employee's budgeting responsibilities within the company, as well as each employee's budgeting responsibilities.

- Make sure the accounting system provides operating reports to assist in the planning process (such as product mix, gross profit reports by units, variance reports, and cash flows) in addition to the standard set of financial statements (balance sheet and income statement).
- Set up the budgets using the same structure that your company uses to accumulate historical data. This practice ensures comparability and facilitates analysis.
- Review the budget to assure that it complies with the firm's overall business objectives.
- Create flexibility in the budgeting process so you can adjust quickly to unexpected conditions in the marketplace. Review the budget periodically to adapt it to new developments (such as increased prices, changed financial and economic conditions, or other changes in the assumptions under which you developed the original plan). When you change the budget, however, be sure to retain the original budget for reference.
- Prepare three budgets using the following projections: most likely, optimistic, and pessimistic. If and when market conditions change, the company will be able to quickly adjust to the level of operations required to survive or to maximize opportunities. Changes in volume typically require staff adjustments. Planning for those adjustments before a market booms or sours results in better and faster decisions and implementation

## Budget Elements

Figure 14.1 illustrates the budgeting process and the relationship among the different components of the profit plan. The series of schedules that follow will take you, step-by-step, through the budgeting process. Each schedule represents a component to incorporate into the overall profit plan.

### Sales Plan

Figure 14.2, schedule 1, developing a sales plan—closings, is the first step in the budgeting process. The sales manager (who also may be the builder, remodeler, or developer) generally is the best qualified to determine sales volume and product mix. He or she should evaluate the market, project market share, and recommend the sales volume and mix for the coming year. If your firm has a production manager, maintain close communication with that person because production capacity can constrain the sales plan. For example, a company cannot sell more units, remodeling jobs, or lots than it is able to produce. Therefore, convert the sales plan into a closing plan based upon your company's cycle time and closing dates.

### Production Plan

The production plan comprises a group of budgets representing the land and land development plan and direct construction costs (fig. 14.3, schedule 2).

Construction cost estimates are essential to the general financial plan of a building company. They provide a yardstick for builders, remodelers, and developers to use to evalate actual performance. Direct construction costs consumes from 50 to 68% of a building company's total sales revenue and 50% of a remodeling company's sales revenue. Development costs including land acquisition (28%) and

**Figure 14.1** Planning information flow

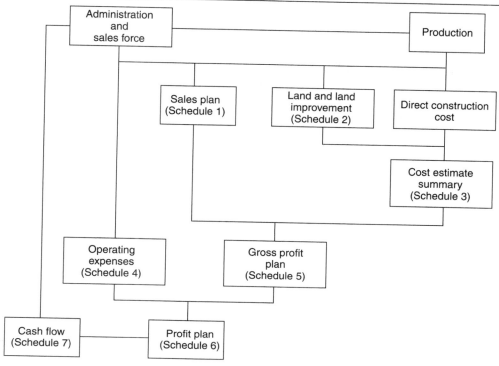

development costs (35%) consume more than 60% of a developer's total sales revenue. Therefore, these three functions have the most impact on a company's ability to meet its profit goals.

The only way to ensure that a construction cost is in line with an estimate is to compare the two as work progresses. Using the same cost codes to accumulate

**Figure 14.2** Schedule 1, sales plan—closings

Date prepared:

| | January | | February | | March | | Quarter total | | Year total | |
|---|---|---|---|---|---|---|---|---|---|---|
| | Units | Amount | Units | Amount | Units | Amount | Units | Amount | Units | Amount |
| 3050 Sales, developed lots | | | | | | | | | | |
| Average sales price | | | | | | | | | | |
| | | | | | | | | | | |
| 3100 Sales, single family | | | | | | | | | | |
| Average sales price | | | | | | | | | | |
| | | | | | | | | | | |
| Total sales revenue | | | | | | | | | | |
| Record schedule 4 | | | | | | | | | | |

Figure 14.3  Schedule 2, land and land improvement plan (prepare monthly)

Date prepared:

|  | Parcel A | Parcel B | Total |
|---|---|---|---|
| 1320    Land held for development | | | |
| 1420    Land and land development cost | | | |
|      Financing and interest | | | |
|      Real estate taxes | | | |
|      Land planning | | | |
|      Engineering | | | |
|      Rough grading | | | |
|      Streets | | | |
|      Curbs and gutters | | | |
|      Sidewalks | | | |
|      Storm sewers, drainage | | | |
|      Sanitary sewers | | | |
|      Water | | | |
|      Electricity and gas | | | |
|      Amenities | | | |
|      Other | | | |
| Total | | | |
| A.  Total cost of land developed | | | |
| B.  Number of lots | | | |
| C.  Cost of finished lots | | | |

construction costs as for estimates simplifies these comparisons. Thus, each cost code becomes a control point as discussed in Chapter 9.

### Land and Land Development Costs

To derive an average cost per lot, builders and developers should accumulate the projected land and land development costs by parcel, then divide the total cost by the number of lots in each parcel (fig. 14.3, schedule 2). Computing unit cost, as illustrated in schedule 2, assumes that all lots in the parcel share land and land development costs in equal proportion. Although this method is the simplest one; Chapter 15 offers other options. Refer to Chapter 12 for a discussion of special considerations in land development. When budgeting for the lot costs in a home building operation, use the market value of the lots instead of the cost to distinguish construction profits from land development profits/losses.

### Direct Construction Costs

Builders, remodelers, and developers should budget direct construction costs in detail for each unit, job, or lot. If they do not know the types of units to be built during the year, they can use the historical direct cost percentage (or the percentage estimated as a target for the year). As units go into production, they would prepare a detailed estimate for each unit.

### Cost Estimate Summary

The cost estimate summary accumulates construction cost categories to show the total cost for units closed each month (fig. 14.4, schedule 3).

### Gross Profit Plan

The gross profit plan integrates the sales and production plans (fig. 14.5, schedule 4). The gross profit plan establishes the contribution each product line will contribute when sold, by subtracting the estimated cost from the proposed sales revenue.

### Operating Expenses Plan

Budget indirect construction costs for the entire operation for the year, allocate them to production units based on the percentage of total estimated indirect construction costs to total estimated direct construction costs, or treat them as an operating expense. For better management control, treat the indirect construction costs as an operating expense and make the required adjustments at the end of the

---

**Figure 14.4**  Schedule 3, cost estimate summary (prepare monthly)

---

Date prepared:

| Cost element | January | February | March | Quarter total | Year total |
|---|---|---|---|---|---|
| 1420  Finished lots at cost (schedule 2) | | | | | |
| | | | | | |
| 1430  Direct construction cost | | | | | |
|     Finished lot cost (at builder's retail) | | | | | |
|     Direct construction cost<br>      (historical or target %) | | | | | |
| | | | | | |
| | | | | | |
| | | | | | |
| Total cost (Record schedule 4 and 6) | | | | | |

**Figure 14.5** Schedule 4, gross profit plan by product line (prepare monthly)

Date prepared:

| | January | February | March | Quarter totals | Year total |
|---|---|---|---|---|---|
| Lots (sales to third parties) | | | | | |
| | | | | | |
| 3050  Sales, developed lots | | | | | |
| 3550  Cost of sales, developed lots | | | | | |
| Gross profit | | | | | |
| Houses: | | | | | |
| 3100  Sales, single-family spec. | | | | | |
| 3600  Cost of sales, single-family spec. | | | | | |
| Finished lot cost | | | | | |
| Direct construction cost | | | | | |
| Gross profit | | | | | |
| | | | | | |
| Total gross profit (Record schedule 6) | | | | | |

NOTE: Sales figures are transferred from schedule 1, cost of sales figures are from schedule 6.

accounting period. Refer to Chapter 7 for more information on how to account for indirect construction costs.

The operating expenses plan estimates the company's nonconstruction expenses, commonly known as operating expenses (fig. 14.6, schedule 5). Operating expenses include indirect construction cost, sales and marketing, financing, and general and administrative expenses. You should budget operating expenses by accounting period rather than allocate them to units closed. In addition, resist the temptation to work with an annual number divided by 12 to arrive at the monthly expense. Instead budget expenses in the month in which they are most likely to occur. Otherwise, your comparisons of budgeted with actual expenses will show variances where none exist.

As with the cost estimates, the budgets need to mirror the accounts that you use to collect the actual numbers. This practice ensures comparability and facilitates the control process.

### Profit Plan

The profit plan portrays the results of company operations during a projected period (fig. 14.7, schedule 6). It is a numerical representation of the company's goals and objectives for the next calendar or fiscal period. The combined efforts of the owner, sales manager, production manager, and general administration provide the

**Figure 14.6** Schedule 5, operating expenses plan (prepare monthly)

Date prepared:

| | January | February | March | Quarter totals | Year total |
|---|---|---|---|---|---|
| 4000  Indirect construction cost | | | | | |
| 4000  Salaries and wages | | | | | |
| 4100  Payroll taxes and benefits | | | | | |
| 4200  Field office expenses | | | | | |
| 4300  Field warehouse and storage | | | | | |
| 4400  Construction vehicles, travel, and entertainment | | | | | |
| 4500  Construction equipment | | | | | |
| 4600  Unsold units and units under construction | | | | | |
| 4700  Warranty and customer service | | | | | |
| 4800  Depreciation expenses | | | | | |
| 4900  Other | | | | | |
| Total indirect construction cost (report schedule 6) | | | | | |
| 5000  Financing expenses | | | | | |
| 5020  Interest on notes payable | | | | | |
| 5040  Interest expense, other | | | | | |
| 5120  Points and fees | | | | | |
| 5130  Appraisal and related fees | | | | | |
| 5140  Inspection fees | | | | | |
| 5210  Closing costs | | | | | |
| 5220  Title and recording | | | | | |
| 5230  Fees, commitment | | | | | |
| Total financing expenses (Record schedule 6) | | | | | |
| 6000  Sales and Marketing | | | | | |
| 6000  Sales salaries and commissions | | | | | |
| 6100  Payroll taxes and benefits | | | | | |
| 6200  Sales office expenses | | | | | |
| 6300  Advertising and sales promotion | | | | | |

*(continued)*

**Figure 14.6** Schedule 5, operating expenses plan (prepare monthly) (continued)

| | January | February | March | Quarter totals | Year total |
|---|---|---|---|---|---|
| 6400 Sales vehicles, travel, and entertainment | | | | | |
| 6600 Model home maintenance | | | | | |
| 6700 Sales and marketing fees | | | | | |
| 6800 Depreciation | | | | | |
| 6900 Marketing expenses, other | | | | | |
| Total Sales and Marketing (Record schedule 7) | | | | | |
| 8000 General and Administrative (G&A) | | | | | |
| 8000 Salaries and wages | | | | | |
| 8100 Payroll taxes and benefits | | | | | |
| 8200 Office expenses | | | | | |
| 8300 Computer expenses | | | | | |
| 8400 Vehicles, travel, and entertainment | | | | | |
| 8500 Taxes | | | | | |
| 8600 Insurance | | | | | |
| 8700 Professional services | | | | | |
| 8800 Depreciation expenses | | | | | |
| 8900 G&A, other | | | | | |
| Total G&A expenses (Record schedule 6) | | | | | |
| Total operating expenses | | | | | |

figures presented in the profit plan. The data appears in a summarized form in Schedule 6, and Schedules 1 to 5 back up the data.

Schedule 6 refers to the schedules from which you obtained the data. In some small-volume companies, the sales and production managers are the same person. In others, the builder, remodeler, or developer might be the sales manager, the production manager, or both. In large companies, different people probably staff the sales, production, and administration functions with the owner's oversight.

### Cash Flow Report

The cash flow report (fig. 14.8, schedule 7) is a powerful tool that builders, remodelers, or developers can use for cash planning and control. It identifies all sources and uses of cash and predicts the period in which the company will receive or need cash.

**Figure 14.7** Schedule 6, profit plan (prepare monthly)

Date prepared:

| | January | February | March | Quarter totals | Year total |
|---|---|---|---|---|---|
| 3000  Sales (schedule 1) | | | | | |
| 3500  Cost of sales (schedule 3) | | | | | |
| Gross profit (schedule 4) | | | | | |
| Operating expenses | | | | | |
| 4000  Indirect construction cost (schedule 5) | | | | | |
| Total operating expenses | | | | | |
| | | | | | |
| Net operating profit or loss | | | | | |
| | | | | | |
| 9100  Other income | | | | | |
| 8300  Other expense | | | | | |
| | | | | | |
| Net income or loss before income tax | | | | | |

NOTE: The income tax provisions depend upon the organizational structure of the company (sole proprietorship, partnership, type of corporation, and so on).

The primary purpose for preparing a cash flow projection is to illustrate the transfer of cash (rather than record the financial transaction). For example, signing an option contract or closing a sales contract does not determine when a company will receive cash. In some areas of the country, a cash transfer occurs several days after closing. In cash planning, this lag can be significant. Similarly, the date you purchase items is unimportant; the crucial date is when you must pay the invoices.

Use the bottom section of the report to plan the company's cash needs. Determine the minimum cash balance needed at the end of every month. In the event of a projected shortage, plan to secure an operating line of credit from a lender. When excess cash is projected, plan how much of the outstanding operating loan to pay.

The ending cash balance for every month becomes the beginning cash balance for the following month. A cash flow report (included in your presentation to a lender) helps the lender decide whether or not to grant your company a loan. It not only shows your company's cash needs, it also shows the company's excess cash or when a loan will be paid. Lenders like to know when they will be paid.

Builders, remodelers, and developers that operate on relatively small cash balances may want to prepare weekly cash flow reports. Businesses with large cash reserves might require cash flow reports only on a monthly basis. Chapter 8 offers additional information about cash flow analysis.

**Figure 14.8** Schedule 7, cash flow (prepare monthly)

Date prepared:

|  | January | February | March | Quarter totals | Year total |
|---|---|---|---|---|---|
| Beginning cash balance |  |  |  |  |  |
|  |  |  |  |  |  |
| Sources of cash |  |  |  |  |  |
| Cash sales |  |  |  |  |  |
| Collection on receivables |  |  |  |  |  |
| Deposits by customers |  |  |  |  |  |
| Construction loans |  |  |  |  |  |
| Total receipts |  |  |  |  |  |
| Total available cash |  |  |  |  |  |
|  |  |  |  |  |  |
| Uses of cash |  |  |  |  |  |
| Payment of accounts payable |  |  |  |  |  |
| Payroll, net |  |  |  |  |  |
| Payroll taxes |  |  |  |  |  |
| Construction loans |  |  |  |  |  |
| Income taxes |  |  |  |  |  |
| Real estate taxes |  |  |  |  |  |
| Land purchases |  |  |  |  |  |
| Interest |  |  |  |  |  |
| Total disbursements |  |  |  |  |  |
| Cash balance |  |  |  |  |  |
| Minimum cash requirement |  |  |  |  |  |
| Cash excess or shortage |  |  |  |  |  |
| Operating cash loans |  |  |  |  |  |
| Loans for operating cash |  |  |  |  |  |
| Borrowed funds needed |  |  |  |  |  |
| Repayment of borrowed funds |  |  |  |  |  |
| Ending loan balance |  |  |  |  |  |
| Ending cash balance |  |  |  |  |  |

### Reports

The greatest benefit of financial planning is being able to use the budgets created throughout the planning process as a yardstick to measure performance.

Reports should compare results with plans or budgets for the same period. Financial reports will be more effective if they meet the following goals:

- Allow owners or managers to measure the performance of each function of the company and relate it to the manager responsible for each function

- Provide timely information that allows builders, remodelers, and developers to act quickly to correct any unfavorable developments indicated by the reports

- Compare results with the plan or budget for each line item on the report

- Highlight deviations from the plan

- Are dependable, accurate, and easy to use (Wherever possible, standardize the format of the reports to facilitate comparison and analysis)

- Allow customization to meet management needs (In large companies, top managers should receive summary reports. Lower-level managers, who are responsible for achieving specific goals, should get detailed reports that back up the summaries. Top managers also receive detailed information upon request)

- Provide benefits that outweigh the cost of preparing the reports

# Technical Aspects of Accounting

This chapter discusses often misunderstood aspects of the accounting system for builders, remodelers, and developers. It outlines GAAP and IRS requirements as well as NAHB policies that were current at press time. Because tax laws are subject to rapid and frequent change, you should consult a qualified accountant or tax expert with questions about the current requirements.

## Acquisition and Development

Special accounting rules pertain to the recording of pre-acquisition, acquisition, and development costs. The rules presented here follow the guidelines provided by AICPA with direct reference to the documentation supporting the rules.

### Pre-Acquisition Costs

Builders and developers often incur costs related to a property prior to taking title to it. These pre-acquisition costs include options to purchase, engineering and architectural fees, and expenses for feasibility study expenses.

You must capitalize the pre-acquisition costs of purchasing a tract or parcel of land—add construction financing expenses to the cost of units built—if the costs are to meet the four basic criteria of Financial Accounting Standards Board (FASB), *Statement of Financial Accounting Standards No. 67*, pgf. 4, as follows:

You can directly connect the pre-acquisition costs with a specific project.

- If your company had already acquired the property, you would capitalize these costs.

- Acquisition of the property is probable.[2]

- The total capitalized costs do not exceed the net realizable value of the property.

Initially, developers should accumulate these costs in account 1320, land held for development. They should debit 1410, land and land development, when land development begins; and credit 1320, and expense any costs that do not meet these criteria. If a firm eventually abandons a project, it would expense all previously capitalized costs related to that acquisition attempt.

### Acquisition Costs

Land acquisition costs include purchase price, legal fees, sales commission, appraisals, recording and other closing fees; engineering, zoning and planning costs; and interest (if it carries a mortgage note). Your company should capitalize all land acquisition to the cost basis of the land. A firm may hold a parcel of land for "investment," future opportunities, land banking, or for any other reason that delays development of the parcel. In these situations, for bookkeeping and tax purposes, expense interest on the acquisition loan and other carrying costs after the firm begins to develop the parcel.

Although costs are accumulated initially in account 1320, when development begins, transfer these costs to 1410 by debiting 1410 and crediting 1320.

If you acquire a tract of land for development, but later decide not to develop it, you must take two steps. First, compare the total cost of the land to the estimated realizable net value of the land, and second, expense the cost in excess of value in the current accounting period. Currently, IRS does not allow a write-off for the cost in excess of value until you have realized the loss. Consult with a reputable tax professional to assure your firm's compliance with all tax regulations.

### Land Development Costs

Land development costs include planning, design, and engineering studies, earthwork (grading, excavation, etc.); utility line installation; streets; curbs; gutters; and sidewalks. (See Appendix G, Land Development Costs, Subsidiary Ledger.)

Costs that can be identified with land must be capitalized. Initially, you would accumulate these costs in 1410, land and land development. Upon completing each tract, debit a pro rata share of costs for each lot to 1420, developed lots, and credit 1410. Determining the pro rata share for individual lots or phases of projects requires an allocation method. FASB, *Statement No. 67*, states that whenever possible, the direct allocation should identify the individual component of construction.[3] When identifying it is not practical, (for example, in subdivision tract acquisition and development), allocate land costs to each component (lot or tract phase) of the project and base the allocation on one of the following methods:

- The fair market value of the land after development but before construction (Determine fair market value at the time of allocation. If assigning a fair market value at this stage of the project is difficult. Pgf. 11 permits allocation of capitalized costs based on area methods.)
- The square-footage-allocation method (Fig. 15.1 is a representative example of this most-often-used method of allocating land development costs.)

At each lot closing, the pro rata calculation produces the amount to be transferred from 1420, developed lots, to 3550, cost of sales, developed lots, or to the appropriate cost of sales account (3500–3700), depending on the type of lot closed.

### Accounting for Amenities

FASB, *Statement No. 67*, pgf. 8, states that the costs of amenities such as swimming pools, clubhouses, workout facilities, golf courses, and tennis courts may be accounted for in one of two ways, depending upon the builder's or developer's in-

**Figure 15.1** Minimum initial investment

| Type of property | Minimum investment (percentage of sales) |
|---|---|
| Single-family residential property | |
| • Primary residence of buyer | 5% |
| • Secondary or recreational residence | 10 |
| Land | |
| • Held for residential development to commence within two years of sale | 20 |
| • Held for residential development to commence after two years | 25 |
| Multifamily residential property | |
| • Primary residence | |
| Cash flow sufficient to service debt | 10 |
| Start up situation or insufficient cash flow to service debt | 15 |
| • Secondary or recreational residence | |
| Cash flow sufficient to service debt | 15 |
| Start up situation or insufficient cash flow to service debt | 25 |

tent. If the amenity is to be turned over to the home owner's association as a "common element" at a later date, allocate the costs of construction to units as they are sold. If you plan to sell the amenity or retain title to it, allocate to the individual units only the costs in excess of fair market value.

Frequently, you must estimate costs because the amenities are not always complete when units are ready for settlement. You must accrue these estimated costs to complete the amenities as a liability and debit them to inventory. At closing, transfer the inventory to cost of sales and include a pro rata share of the unfinished work.[4]

### Carrying Costs

Some people in the building industry are confused about how to account for general carrying charges, including interest, other financing costs, and property taxes. In both methods (fair market value and square-footage allocation), many builders and developers capitalize these costs until the construction period is complete. After this point, you can either capitalize them or expense them in accordance with IRS guidelines.

## Direct Construction Costs

Direct construction costs include permits, labor, materials, trade contractors, construction period interest, and any other costs directly related to construction of a particular job or unit. The NAHB Chart of Accounts accumulates these costs in 1430, direct construction cost. A subsidiary ledger summarizing construction costs for each unit must support this account. Please refer to Appendix E, which contains a sample chart of accounts for the direct construction costs, subsidiary ledger.

Upon completing a unit, credit 1430 and debit 1510, finished units. Upon closing the unit, credit 1510 and debit the appropriate costs of sales account.

Builders who develop their own lots should segregate lot and structure costs. Carefully accumulating these costs helps builders monitor variances from budgeted estimates and enables them to measure strengths and weaknesses of land development and construction operations.

FASB, *Statement No. 67*, pgf. 7, addresses the accounting requirements for direct and indirect construction costs as follows:

> Project costs clearly associated with the acquisition, development, and construction of a real estate project shall be capitalized as a cost of that project. Indirect project costs that relate to several projects shall be capitalized and allocated to the projects to which the costs relate. Indirect costs that do not clearly relate to projects under development or construction, including general and administrative expenses, shall be charged to expense as incurred.[5]

## Indirect Construction Costs

Accumulate indirect costs in 1440, indirect construction cost, and support the account with a subsidiary ledger summarizing the indirect construction costs for a project or period, whichever is appropriate. Appendix F provides the NAHB-recommended outline of a subsidiary chart of accounts for indirect construction costs. To help manage costs, many builders prefer to accumulate indirect costs as operating expenses while the expenses are being incurred (NAHB Chart of Accounts, 4000 series). For either method, to conform to IRS and GAAP requirements, you eventually must allocate all indirect construction costs to a specific unit of production such as a house, a remodeling job, or a lot.

The principle behind spreading or allocating indirect costs to individual units of production is to determine (as accurately as possible) the gross profit on each unit sold. Often, the most practical procedure is to estimate the indirect construction costs at the beginning of a project or phase and allocate the estimated amount to each unit. At the end of the fiscal period or upon project completion, reconcile the actual indirect costs with the allocated estimate and adjust for variances at the end of the accounting period.

If your firm chooses to use the 4000 series of accounts and expense indirect construction costs as it incurs them, gross profit would not include indirect construction cost. Manage the group of accounts for indirect construction cost similarly to the other three groups of accounts: financing, sales and marketing, and general and administrative expenses. To conform to IRS and GAAP requirements, allocate a portion of the cost accumulated in the 4000 series to 1440, indirect construction costs, in the asset group of accounts. Do this allocation monthly, quarterly, or at the end of the calendar or fiscal year.

Builders, remodelers, and developers must look at their operations to determine the best allocation method for their businesses. The following paragraphs describe the five major methods of allocating indirect construction costs to costs of sales:

**Figure 15.2** Sales value

| | No. of units | Estimated sales value | Percent of total |
|---|---|---|---|
| Model A | 5 | $ 500,000 | 22% |
| Model B | 10 | 800,000 | 35 |
| Model C | 15 | 975,000 | 43 |
| Total | | $ 2,275,000 | 100 |

| | Total indirect costs | | Percent of total | | Group total ÷ units | | Indirect costs per unit |
|---|---|---|---|---|---|---|---|
| Model A | $ 300,000 | × | .22 | = | $ 66,000 ÷ 5 | = | $ 13,200 |
| Model B | 300,000 | × | .35 | = | 105,000 ÷ 10 | = | 10,500 |
| Model C | 300,000 | × | .43 | = | 129,000 ÷ 15 | = | 8,600 |

*Sales Value*

Builders often use this method when selling several different models (plans) in the same subdivision. To use this method

1. Determine the number of units in the subdivision and the estimated sales value of each group of homes. Compare that value with the total estimated sales value of the subdivision to determine the percentage of total sales for each model group.
2. Multiply the percentage by total indirect construction costs to determine the allocation of indirect costs to each group of homes.
3. Calculate the indirect costs for each unit within a model group and divide the total indirect costs for a group by the number of units in the group (fig. 15.2).

*Number of Units Built*

Using this method, divide the total indirect costs by the total number of units built to determine an average indirect cost per unit. This method works accurately only if you are building the same or similar house plans (fig. 15.3).

**Figure 15.3** Number of units built

$$\frac{\text{Total indirect costs}}{\text{Units to be built}} = \frac{\$300,000}{30} = \$10,000 \text{ allocation to each unit}$$

*Total Direct Costs*

To use this popular method, divide the total estimated direct cost of the unit by the total direct costs for all units built. The result is the percentage of the each individual unit's contribution to total direct costs. Multiply this percentage by the total indirect construction costs for all the units to calculate the indirect cost for each unit (fig.15.4).

**Figure 15.4** Total direct costs

$$\frac{\text{Total direct costs of unit 1}}{\text{Cost of units to be built}} = \frac{\$50,000}{\$1,000,000} = 0.05\ (5\%)$$

| | |
|---|---|
| Total indirect costs | $ 300,000 |
| Unit % of total direct costs | × 0.05 (5%) |
| Allocation to unit 1 | $ 15,000 |

### Area
Builders and developers often use the area method in subdivisions with units that vary in area. First, divide the total estimated indirect construction costs by the total area in sq. ft. of all a project's units to get the cost per sq. ft. Next, multiply cost per sq. ft. by the actual number of sq. ft. in each unit. These calculations produce the indirect cost to allocate for each unit (fig. 15.5).

**Figure 15.5** Area

$$\frac{\text{Total estimated indirect costs}}{\text{Area of all units (sq. ft.)}} = \frac{\$300,000}{45,000} = \$6.67/\text{sq. ft.}$$

| | |
|---|---|
| Total area of unit 1 | 2,000 sq. ft. |
| Indirect cost per foot | × $6.67 |
| Allocated to unit 1 | $ 13,340 |

### Percent of Indirect to Direct Cost
This popular calculation method establishes a percentage of indirect costs to direct costs. Calculate the allocation as a percentage of dollars spent for direct costs in each unit (fig. 5.6).

**Figure 5.6** Percent of indirect to direct cost

$$\frac{\text{Total estimated indirect costs}}{\text{Total estimated direct costs}} = \frac{\$90,000}{\$1,000,000} = 0.09\ (9\%)$$

| | |
|---|---|
| Total direct costs of unit 1 | $ 50,000 |
| Times percentage of indirect cost | × 0.09 (9%) |
| Indirect cost allocation to unit 1 | $ 4,500 |

### IRS Requires Consistency
A builder who repeatedly builds the same model might prefer the method using the number of units built; whereas a builder with a diverse product line might choose the method using the percentage of direct construction costs; and a multifamily builder probably would use the area method. In any case, consistency is the most important requirement for meeting IRS "reasonable" allocation standards. Therefore, when making year-end adjustments to correct estimates of indirect costs, use the same allocation method used during the year. Also strive for consistency among your projects.

## Sales and Marketing Expenses

Under certain circumstances, builders, remodelers, and developers must capitalize some sales and marketing costs. These costs must meet two criteria outlined in FASB, *Statement Standard No. 67*, pgf. 17, as follows: (1) you must reasonably expect to recover the costs, and (2) the costs must relate to a tangible asset that your firm uses throughout the sales period (for example, brochures and signs).[6]

Model homes and their furnishings, sales facilities, and semi-permanent signs are examples of capitalized sales and marketing costs. Marketing and sales costs to be expensed as incurred include advertising, salesperson overhead (including salaries and fringe benefits), and promotion of gala events.

## Revenue Recognition

FASB, *Statement No. 66*, Real Estate Sales Other Than Retail Land Sales, provides insight into applying GAAP in accounting for revenues from sales of the following:

- a home, building, or parcel of land
- lots to builders
- options to acquire real estate
- time-sharing interests in real estate
- corporate stock or partnership interests in which the transaction is actually a real estate transfer

GAAP requires that revenue be realized in the period in which earnings are substantially complete, and money and property have been exchanged. Builders usually recognize the amount established by the parties to the exchange, except when the seller is not reasonably sure of collecting the receivables. An explanation of accepted methods of accounting for revenue recognition follows.

### Full Accrual

Under the full accrual method, recognize revenue at the time of sale. It is often mistakenly called the completed-contract method. However, that method requires recognizing revenue when a contract is considered complete or substantially complete. The full accrual method is a modified completed-contract approach, which allows revenues and expenses to be "matched" in the same time period.

Because the full accrual method requires recognizing all revenue at closing, all related costs accrue in the cost of sales account for the same period. If a unit is partially completed at year end, the related costs remain in inventory with no recognized revenue. If a completed unit remains unsold at the end of a period, the costs stay in account 1510, finished units. Again, you would not recognize any revenue.

You have consummated a sale when you and the buyer have met all conditions preceding closing (including arrangement of permanent financing by the buyer), you and the buyer have exchanged all considerations related to the sale, and you have legally passed the title to the buyer.

The full accrual method has one exception that allows you to recognize income prior to the closing of a sale. To qualify for this exception, you must meet two criteria as follows: (1) you must be able to determine the amount of profit your company will earn and be reasonably sure you will collect it, and (2) the work must be substantially complete.

To use the full accrual method for the normal closing of a residential unit, you must meet the following three basic criteria:

1. You must close a sale.
2. The buyer's investment must be sufficient to demonstrate a commitment to pay for the property.
3. You, the seller, must have transferred the usual risks and rewards of ownership to the buyer. The seller must not have a substantial continuing involvement with the property

The usual risks and rewards of ownership are transferred when the seller no longer has a substantial continuing interest in the property or when all of the contract obligations have been met. Full performance removes the seller's receivable, if one exists, from possible future subordination to any other lien holder.

## Percentage of Completion

In the percentage-of-completion method, you should recognize income throughout the life of a project contract based upon a periodic (usually annual) measurement of progress toward completion. Obviously, this method can work well for builders of commercial and industrial projects that take longer than single-family houses to complete, but it has limited application for home builders.

FASB, *Statement No. 66,* permits using this method with high-rise condominium and time-share units. Revenue recognition for low-rise condominiums differs from that for high-rise condominiums because builders can complete a low-rise, cluster condominium and obtain a certificate of occupancy for it before substantially completing the rest of the subdivision. For these low-rise projects, use the full accrual method and recognize the profit at the time of closing.

FASB, *Statement No. 66,* addresses the percentage-of-completion method as follows:

> The earnings process is not complete if a seller is obliged to complete improvements of lots sold or to construct amenities and other facilities applicable to lots sold, if those obligations are significant in relation to total costs, and if they remain unperformed at the time the sale is recognized. Therefore, the amount of revenue recognized at the time of sale is measured by the relationship of costs already incurred to total estimated costs to be incurred, including costs of the marketing effort.[7]

Pgf. 75 states that estimated costs are based upon costs generally expected in the local construction market, so review these estimates at least annually. Changes in estimates do not lead to adjustment of revenue previously recorded unless the adjusted total cost exceeds applicable revenue.[8]

## Other Sources of Information

This chapter is intended to clarify some of the more confusing issues of accounting for home builders, remodelers, and developers. For additional information, contact your accountant or call the NAHB Business Management Department. It maintains a list of industry financial consultants who can assist builders with many of their accounting and financial management needs. Also refer to www.irs.gov and www.fasb.org for more information.

# Part A Outline of NAHB Chart of Accounts

## 1000–1990 Assets

### 1000–1090 Cash
1010 Petty cash
1020 Cash on deposit, general
1030 Cash on deposit, payroll
1040 Cash on deposit, savings and money market
1050 Cash on deposit, held in escrow

### 1100–1190 Short-term Investments
1110 Certificates of deposit
1120 Marketable securities
1130 Government securities
1190 Other short-term investments

### 1200–1290 Receivables
1210 Accounts receivable, trade
1220 Accounts receivable, other
1230 Notes receivable
1250 Mortgage notes receivable, current year
1260 Due on construction and development loans
1265 Costs in excess of billings
1270 Accrued interest receivable
1280 Allowance for doubtful accounts
1290 Retentions (retainage) receivable

### 1300–1390 Inventories
1310 Construction materials inventory
1320 Land held for development
1330 Property held for remodeling

### 1400–1490 Construction Work in Progress
1410 Land and land development
1412 Accumulated allocations, land and land development costs
1420 Developed lots
1425 Reserve for impairment on developed lots
1430 Direct construction cost
1440 Indirect construction cost

### 1500–1590 Finished Units and Other Inventory
1510 Finished units
1520 Model homes
1530 Trade-ins and repossessions

### 1600–1690 Other Current Assets
1610 Refundable deposits
1620 Prepaid expenses
1630 Employee advances
1650 Due from affiliates or subsidiaries
1660 Due from officers, stockholders, owners, or partners
1690 Other current assets

### 1700–1790 Investments and Other Assets
1710 Investments, long-term
1720 Cash surrender value of officers' life insurance
1730 Investments in affiliated entities
1750 Mortgage notes receivable, long-term
1760 Due from affiliated companies or subsidiaries, long-term
1770 Due from officers, owners, stockholders, long-term
1780 Organization cost

### 1800–1890 Property, Plant, and Equipment
1810 Land
1820 Buildings
1825 Rental property
1827 Recreation amenities
1830 Office furniture and equipment
1840 Vehicles
1850 Construction equipment
1870 Model home furnishings
1880 Leasehold improvements
1890 Computer equipment and software

### 1900–1990 Accumulated Depreciation
1920 Accumulated depreciation, buildings
1925 Accumulated depreciation, rental properties
1927 Accumulated depreciation, recreation amenities
1930 Accumulated depreciation, office furniture and equipment
1940 Accumulated depreciation, vehicles
1950 Accumulated depreciation, construction equipment

1970  Accumulated depreciation, model home furnishings
1980  Accumulated depreciation, leasehold improvements
1990  Accumulated depreciation, computer equipment and software

# 2000–2990 Liabilities and Owners' Equity

### 2000–2090 Deposits by Customers
2010  Contract deposits
2030  Tenant security deposit
2040  Advance rent collected

### 2100–2190 Accounts Payable
2110  Accounts payable, trade
2120  Retentions payable
2190  Accounts payable, other

### 2200–2290 Notes Payable
2200  Line of credit payable
2220  Acquisitions and development loans payable
2230  Construction loans payable
2240  Current portion of long-term debt
2290  Notes payable, other

### 2300–2490 Other Current Liabilities
2310  Social Security and Medicare
2320  Federal payroll tax, withheld and accrued
2330  State payroll tax, withheld and accrued
2340  Other payroll withholdings
2345  Union withholding and benefits payable
2350  Sales and use taxes payable
2360  Real estate taxes payable
2370  Income taxes payable
2390  Accrued interest payable
2400  Accrued salaries and wages payable
2410  Accrued commissions payable
2411  Accrued pension and profit-sharing expenses
2420  Workers' compensation insurance payable
2425  Other accrued expenses
2430  Deferred income
2440  Due to affiliated companies or subsidiaries
2450  Due to officers, stockholders, owners, partners
2480  Billings in excess of costs
2490  Other current liabilities

### 2500–2890 Long-term Liabilities
2510  Long-term notes payable
2530  Mortgage notes payable
2600  Deferred income tax payable
2610  Due to affiliated companies or subsidiaries, long-term

2620 Due to officers, stockholders, owners, partners, long-term
2700 Other long-term liabilities

### 2900–2990 *Owners' Equity*
2900 Common Stock
2910 Additional Paid in Capital
2920 Retained Earnings
2930 Treasury stock
2940 Unrealized holding loss
2950 Partnership or proprietorship account
2960 Distributions, dividends, and draws

# 3000–3990 Sales, Revenues, and Cost of Sales

### 3000–3490 *Sales and Revenues*
3000 Sales, land held for development
3050 Sales, developed lots
3100 Sales, single-family, speculative
3110 Sales, single-family, production
3120 Sales, single-family, custom designed
3125 Sales, single-family, custom, no land
3130 Sales, residential remodeling
3133 Sales, commercial and industrial remodeling
3135 Sales, insurance restoration
3137 Sales, repairs
3140 Sales, multifamily
3150 Sales, commercial and industrial
3160 Sales, trade-ins, repossessions
3190 Sales, other
3195 Cancellation fees
3200 Rental property income
3210 Common area reimbursements
3220 Other reimbursements
3230 Parking fee income
3240 Amenities and facilities income
3360 Construction management fee income
3370 Design fees collected
3400 Miscellaneous income
3410 Interest income
3420 Dividend income
3450 Earned discounts
3460 Earned rebates
3490 Sales concessions and discounts

### 3500–3700 *Cost of Sales*
3500 Cost of sales, land held for development
3550 Cost of sales, developed lots
3600 Cost of sales, single-family, speculative

3610 Cost of sales, single-family, production
3620 Cost of sales, single-family, custom designed
3625 Cost of sales, single family, custom, no land
3630 Cost of sales, remodeling
3633 Cost of sales, commercial and industrial remodeling
3635 Cost of sales, insurance restoration
3637 Cost of sales, repairs
3640 Cost of sales, multifamily
3650 Cost of sales, commercial and industrial
3660 Cost of sales, trade-ins
3690 Cost of sales, other
3700 Direct construction cost for prior periods

### 3800–3899 Costs of Construction—Remodeling

3810 Direct labor
3820 Labor burden
3830 Building material
3840 Trade contractors
3850 Rental equipment
3860 Other direct construction costs
3870 Professional design fees

# 4000–4990 Indirect Construction Cost

### 4000–4090 Salaries and Wages

4010 Superintendents
4020 Laborers
4030 Production manager
4040 Architects, drafters, estimators, purchasers
4050 Warranty and customer service manager
4060 Warranty and customer service wages
4070 Other indirect construction wages

### 4100–4190 Payroll Taxes and Benefits

4110 Payroll taxes
4120 Workers' compensation insurance
4130 Health and accident insurance
4140 Retirement, pension, profit sharing
4150 Union benefits
4190 Other benefits

### 4200–4290 Field Office Expenses

4210 Rent, field office
4230 Repairs and maintenance, field office
4250 Utilities, field office
4260 Telephone, field office
4265 Mobile phones, pagers, radios—field
4290 Other field office expenses

### 4300–4390  Field Warehouse and Storage Expenses
4310  Rent, field warehouse and storage
4330  Repairs and maintenance, field warehouse and storage
4350  Utilities, field warehouse and storage
4360  Telephone, field warehouse and storage

### 4400–4490  Construction Vehicles, Travel, and Entertainment
4410  Lease payments, construction vehicles
4420  Mileage reimbursement
4430  Repairs and maintenance, construction vehicles
4440  Operating expenses, construction vehicles
4450  Taxes, licenses, insurance, construction vehicles
4460  Travel, construction department
4470  Customer business entertainment, construction
4480  Training and education, construction
4490  Recruiting fees and expenses, construction

### 4500–4590  Construction Equipment
4510  Rent, construction equipment
4530  Repairs and maintenance, construction equipment
4540  Operating expenses, construction equipment
4550  Taxes and insurance, construction equipment
4560  Small tools and supplies

### 4600–4690  Expenses for Maintaining Unsold Units and Units Under Construction
4610  Temporary utilities
4620  Trash maintenance
4640  Lawn care
4650  Utilities, completed units
4660  Repairs and maintenance, completed units

### 4700–4790  Warranty and Customer Service
4710  Salaries and wages, warranty
4720  Material, warranty
4730  Trade contractor, warranty
4790  Other, warranty expenses

### 4800–4890  Depreciation Expenses
4820  Depreciation, construction office
4830  Depreciation, warehouse
4840  Depreciation, construction vehicles
4850  Depreciation, construction equipment

### 4900–4990  Other
4910  Insurance and bonding expenses
4920  Builder's risk insurance
4990  Absorbed indirect costs

# 5000–5990 Financing Expenses

### 5000–5090 Interest

5010 Interest on line of credit
5020 Interest on notes payable
5030 Interest expense on developed lots
5040 Interest incurred on construction loans
5050 Interest on completed speculative inventory
5090 Interest expense, other

### 5100–5190 Construction Loan Points and Fees

5120 Points and fees
5130 Appraisal and related fees
5140 Inspection fees

### 5200–5290 Closing Costs

5210 Closing costs
5220 Title and recording
5230 Loan fees

# 6000–6990 Sales and Marketing Expenses

### 6000–6090 Sales Salaries, Commissions

6010 Compensation, sales manager
6030 Salaries, sales personnel
6040 Sales commissions, in-house
6050 Sales commissions, outside
6090 Other sales office salaries and wages

### 6100–6190 Payroll Taxes and Benefits, Sales and Marketing

6110 Payroll taxes, sales and marketing
6120 Workers' compensation insurance, sales and marketing
6130 Health and accident insurance, sales and marketing
6140 Retirement, pension, profit-sharing plans, sales and marketing
6190 Other benefits, sales and marketing

### 6200–6290 Sales Office Expenses

6210 Rent, sales office
6230 Repairs and maintenance, sales office
6250 Utilities, sales office
6260 Telephone, sales office
6270 Supplies, sales office

### 6300–6390 Advertising and Sales Promotion

6310 Print advertising
6320 Radio advertising
6325 Television advertising
6330 Internet fees, Web page design and maintenance expense
6340 Brochures and catalogs

6350  Signs
6355  Billboards
6365  Promotions
6370  Agency commissions
6380  Multiple listing fees
6390  Public relations
6395  Referral fees

### 6400–6490  Sales Vehicles, Travel, and Entertainment
6410  Lease payments, sales vehicles
6420  Mileage reimbursement
6430  Repairs and maintenance, sales vehicles
6440  Operating expenses, sales vehicles
6450  Taxes, licenses, insurance, sales vehicles
6460  Travel, sales and marketing
6470  Customer business entertainment

### 6600–6690  Model Home Maintenance
6610  Rent or lease payments, model home furnishings
6620  Model home rent or lease payments
6625  Decorating fees, model homes
6630  Repairs and maintenance, model homes
6650  Utilities, model homes
6670  Lawn and landscaping care, model homes
6680  Cleanup, model homes
6690  Interest on model homes

### 6700–6790  Sales and Marketing Fees
6710  Market research and consultation
6720  Interior design fee
6770  Recruiting fees and expenses, sales and marketing personnel
6780  Training and education expenses

### 6800–6890  Depreciation
6810  Depreciation, sales office
6830  Depreciation, sales vehicles
6870  Depreciation, model home furnishings, decorations

### 6900–6990  Other Marketing Expenses
6930  Sales concessions
6940  Buy downs
6999  Other sales and marketing expenses

# 7000–7990  Operating and Management Expenses, Rental Operations

### 7000–7090  Property Management
7010  Compensation, property manager

7030 Salaries and wages, property management personnel
7040 Commissions, in-house
7050 Commissions, outside
7060 Salaries and wages, maintenance personnel
7070 Payroll taxes and benefits, rental operations
7072 Workers' compensation insurance, rental
7073 Health and accident insurance, rental
7074 Retirement, pension, profit-sharing plans, rental
7079 Other benefits, rental

### 7100–7190 Rental Expenses
7110 Advertising
7130 Credit reports
7190 Other rental expenses

### 7200–7290 Administrative Expenses, Rental Operations
7220 Management and service fees
7230 Office expenses
7240 Telephone
7250 Tenant bad debts
7260 Collection costs
7290 Other administrative expenses

### 7300–7390 Professional Services, Rental Operations
7310 Legal services
7320 Accounting services
7330 Market research
7390 Other professional services, rental operations

### 7400–7490 Operating Expenses, Rental Operations
7410 Utilities
7420 Engineering
7430 Janitorial
7440 Trash removal service
7450 Exterminating
7460 Snow removal
7470 Other contractual services
7480 Vehicles and equipment, rental operations
7490 Other rental operations expenses

### 7500–7590 Taxes and Insurance, Rental Operations
7510 Real estate property taxes
7520 Personal property taxes
7530 Franchise taxes
7540 License fees
7560 Workers' compensation insurance
7570 Insurance, rental operations
7590 Other taxes and insurance, rental operations

### 7600–7690 Maintenance and Repairs, Rental Operations
7610  Tenant redecorating
7630  Maintenance contracts and services
7640  Ground maintenance and repairs
7650  Vehicle maintenance and repairs, rental operations
7660  Equipment maintenance and repairs, rental operations
7670  Amenities maintenance and repairs

### 7700–7790 Financing Expense, Rental Operations
7710  Interest on mortgage payable
7720  Interest on long-term notes payable

### 7800–7890 Depreciation Expenses, Rental Operations
7810  Depreciation, building
7820  Depreciation, maintenance equipment
7830  Depreciation, vehicles
7840  Depreciation, furniture and fixtures
7850  Depreciation, amenities
7890  Other depreciation

### 7900–7990 Other Management and Operating Expenses

## 8000–8990  General and Administrative Expense

### 8000–8090 Salaries and Wages
8010  Salaries, owners
8020  Salaries, officers
8030  Salaries, management
8050  Salaries and wages, office and clerical
8090  Other general and administrative salaries and wages

### 8100–8190 Payroll Taxes and Benefits
8110  Payroll taxes
8120  Workers' compensation insurance
8130  Health and accident insurance
8140  Retirement, pension, profit-sharing plans
8190  Other employee benefits

### 8200–8290 Office Expenses
8210  Rent
8220  Office equipment rental
8230  Repairs and maintenance, administrative office space
8240  Repairs and maintenance, administrative office equipment
8250  Utilities, administrative office
8260  Telephone, administrative office
8270  Office supplies, administrative office
8280  Postage and deliveries
8290  Miscellaneous expenses, administrative office

### 8300–8390  Technology and Computer Expenses
8310  Computer supplies
8320  Leases, computer hardware
8330  Leases, computer software
8335  Software licensing and subscription fees
8340  Network and web development expenses
8350  Repairs and maintenance, computer equipment
8360  Maintenance, computer software

### 8400–8490  Vehicles, Travel, and Entertainment
8410  Lease, administrative vehicles
8420  Mileage reimbursement
8430  Repairs and maintenance, administrative vehicles
8440  Operating expense, administrative vehicles
8450  Taxes, licenses, insurance, administrative vehicles
8460  Travel
8470  Customer business expense
8480  Meeting expenses
8490  In-house meeting expenses

### 8500–8590  Taxes
8510  Sales and use taxes
8520  Real estate taxes
8530  Personal property taxes
8540  License fees
8590  Other taxes

### 8600–8690  Insurance
8610  Hazard insurance, property insurance
8630  General liability insurance
8690  Other insurance

### 8700–8790  Professional Services
8710  Accounting services
8720  Legal services
8730  Consulting services
8770  Recruiting and hiring
8790  Other professional expenses

### 8800–8890  Depreciation Expenses
8810  Depreciation, buildings
8830  Depreciation, vehicles
8840  Depreciation, furniture and equipment
8860  Amortization of leasehold improvements
8870  Depreciation computer equipment and software
8880  Amortization of organization cost
8890  Depreciation, other

*8900–8990  General and Administrative Expense, Other*

8900  Bad debts
8905  Legal settlement expenses
8910  Contributions
8911  Contributions, political
8920  Dues and subscriptions
8950  Bank charges
8960  Penalties and other non-deductible expenses
8990  Training and education expenses

## 9000–9990  Other Income and Expenses

*9100–9190  Other Income*

9100  Income from partnerships, joint ventures, S-corps, and LLCs
9120  Loss from impairment write-downs of developed lots
9150  Gain or loss on sale of assets
9190  Other

## 9200–9290  Other Expenses

## 9200  Extraordinary Expenses

## 9300–9390  Provision for Income Taxes

9300  Provision for federal income taxes
9320  Provision for state income taxes
9330  Provision for local income taxes

# Part B The Complete NAHB Chart of Accounts

## 1000–1990 Assets

### 1000–1090 Cash

**1010 Petty cash**—All of a company's petty cash accounts, whether maintained in office or by construction superintendent in the field

**1020 Cash on deposit, general**—Demand deposits in bank for all regular trade receipts and disbursements

**1030 Cash on deposit, payroll**—Demand deposits in bank for payroll disbursements only (Generally, companies that employ their own crews and write a large number of payroll checks maintain a separate checking account to cover payroll. For each pay period, a check for the total amount of the payroll is written against the general account and deposited into the payroll account.)

**1040 Cash on deposit, savings and money market**—Deposits in savings and money market accounts

**1050 Cash on deposit, held in escrow**—Cash held at title companies, disbursing agents, and financial institutions, representing refundable customer deposits, completion escrows, or other escrowed funds

### 1100–1190 Short-term Investments

**1110 Certificates of deposit**—Funds deposited in interest-bearing certificates of deposit (CDs), maturing in less than one year

**1120 Marketable securities**—Funds invested in readily marketable stock of unaffiliated companies that management intends to dispose of within one year (In accordance with generally accepted accounting principles [GAAP], these investments should be carried at the lower of aggregate cost or market value. To adjust, credit this account and debit 2940, unrealized holding loss.)

**1130 Government securities**—Funds invested in securities issued by federal, state, or local authorities maturing in less than one year

**1190 Other short-term investments**—Funds invested in other instruments for set periods (usually less than one year) that earn interest or dividend income

### 1200–1290 Receivables

**1210 Accounts receivable, trade**—Amounts due to the business for construction, including customers' orders for extras, management services, or other services performed on open account

**1220 Accounts receivable, other**—Amounts due to the business for services not otherwise classified

**1230 Notes receivable**—Unpaid balances due to the company on notes received in full or partial settlement of open or short-term accounts

**1250 Mortgage notes receivable, current year**—Mortgages taken from purchasers in lieu of cash; payments due within 12 months

**1260 Due on construction and development loans**—Amounts due from financial institutions on construction and development loans (The balance of this account represents the amount of cash available from construction and development loans. When a loan is approved, debit this account to show how much cash is available through the loan, and credit 2220, acquisitions and development loans payable, or 2230, construction loans payable. As you draw cash from the loan, you decrease, or credit, 1260, due on construction and development loans, to show how much cash is available to draw from the loan. Alternatively, you can record draws against construction loans directly to account 2220, acquisitions and development loans payable, or 2230, construction loans payable.)

**1265 Costs in excess of billings**—Primarily used by remodelers, custom builders, and commercial builders to record costs that exceed their estimated costs (sometimes referred to as under billing) based upon the percentage of completion method

**1270 Accrued interest receivable**—Interest earned but not received from all sources such as bonds, notes, and mortgages

**1280 Allowance for doubtful accounts**—A contra account that has a credit balance reflecting the potential uncollectible amounts of any account in the receivables classification (A contra account reduces the balance of an account in this case, accounts receivable without changing the account itself.)

**1290 Retentions (retainage) receivable**—Amounts withheld by customers on progress billings. (When retentions become due, debit 1220, accounts receivable other, and credit 1290, retention receivable.)

### 1300–1390 Inventories

**1310 Construction materials inventory**—Control account for book value of construction materials purchased and stored, rather than delivered directly to a job in progress (As materials are allocated to a specific job, the cost is transferred and debited to 1430, direct construction cost, and credited to 1310, construction materials inventory. Excess materials purchased directly for a specific job and originally debited to 1430 should be debited to 1310 and credited to 1430 if the materials are transferred to inventory. Or they should be added to the cost of the house for which the materials are used.)

**1320 Land held for development**—Control account for cost of land purchased for future development (The cost of land increases by recording fees, legal fees, and other acquisition costs. Debit cost of land to 1410, land and land development, at the time the land is to be developed, and credit 1320, land held for development.)

1330 **Property held for remodeling**—Acquisition costs for properties held for future improvement or remodeling (Once the work is completed, they may be sold or held for investment.)

### 1400–1490 Work in Progress

1410 **Land and land development**—Control account for all land and land development costs (see Appendix G) (Cumulative cost of land and land development, including cost of raw land, financing and interest, land planning, engineering, grading, streets, curbs and gutters, sidewalks, storm sewers, temporary utilities, professional fees, permits, and other costs pertaining to the development of the raw land

1412 **Accumulated allocations, land, and land development costs**—Accumulated write-offs to developed lots or to cost of sales for land and land development costs (At the time of closing, debit the cost of the lot to the appropriate cost of sales account in the 3500 to 3700 series and credit 1412.)

1420 **Developed lots**—Cost of lots developed prior to purchase to be used for construction (When a house is closed, debit the cost to the appropriate cost of sales account in the 3500 to 3700 series.)

1425 **Reserve for impairment on developed lots**—Reserve to reflect lower of cost or market value of developed lots

1430 **Direct construction cost**—Control account for all direct construction costs (see Appendix E) including permits, direct labor, materials, trade contractors, equipment rentals and any other direct charge to the units under construction (This account must be supported by a job cost subsidiary detailing the cost of each construction unit. It also includes finance and interest charges during construction. Don't include marketing costs or indirect construction costs in this account. When a house is closed, debit the cost to the appropriate cost of sales account in the 3500 to 3700 series.)

1440 **Indirect construction cost**—A control account that requires a detailed breakdown in a subsidiary ledger showing the different types of cost accumulated in this account (By adding an additional two digits to establish sub accounts, a detailed breakdown of the indirect construction costs can be accommodated in the general chart of accounts [see Appendix F]. Indirect construction costs are necessary costs of building that cannot be directly or easily attributed to a specific house or job. These costs are classified as part of the value of inventories because they contribute to the value of the work in progress. The IRS and GAAP generally require construction inventories to include a proportional share of indirect costs. When a sold house is closed, debit the proportional share of the cost in the 3500 to 3700 series. Alternatively, treat indirect costs by recording the cost within the 4000 series, an operating expense classification. To comply with IRS and GAAP requirements when using the alternative method, allocate the proportional share of indirect construction costs to the 1440 account.)

### 1500–1590 Finished Units and Other Inventory

1510 **Finished units**—Accumulated direct and indirect construction costs of units completed but not sold (Transfer from and credit accounts 1430, direct construction cost, and 1440, indirect construction cost, at the time of completion. The cost of the lot, accumulated in 1420, developed lots, is transferred to the 3500–3700 series at the time the sale is closed.)

**1520 Model homes**—Cost includes lot cost and direct and indirect construction costs of houses used as models (Upon completion of a model, transfer the costs to this account from 1420, developed lots; 1430, direct construction cost; and 1440, indirect construction cost, by debiting account 1520 and crediting accounts 1420, 1430, and 1440 by the respective amounts. Upon sale of model, transfer and debit costs to the 3500–3700 series and credit 1520.)

**1530 Trade-ins and repossessions**—The cost of any trade-ins acquired during a sales transaction and that are held for resale, but not held as investment, including refurbishing until sold (Transfer cost to 3660, cost of sales, trade-ins, when the units are closed.)

### 1600–1690 Other Current Assets

**1610 Refundable deposits**—Deposits paid to and held by municipalities, utilities, and other businesses for performance or completion of operation. (Include refundable plan deposits.)

**1620 Prepaid expenses**—Unexpired portions of expenses applicable to future periods, for items such as insurance, rent, commitment fees, interest and taxes (Detailed accounts for prepayments may be provided by using an additional sub-ledger or adding a two-digit subclass to the main account number.)

**1630 Employee advances**—Debit for a salary advance and credit when advance is deducted from payroll or repaid by employee

**1650 Due from affiliates or subsidiaries**—Short-term receivables due from affiliates or subsidiary companies

**1660 Due from officers, stockholders, owners, or partners**—Amounts currently due from officers, stockholders, owners, or partners of the business

**1690 Other current assets**—Miscellaneous current assets not otherwise classified

### 1700–1790 Investments and Other Assets

**1710 Investments, long-term**—Stocks, bonds, and other securities to be held as long-term investments (By using an additional sub-ledger or two-digit subclass, each type of investment can be maintained in a separate account.)

**1720 Cash surrender value of officers' life insurance**—Accumulated net cash surrender value; net of any outstanding loans on life insurance carried on the officers of the business

**1730 Investments in affiliated entities**—Capital stock of affiliated companies, subsidiaries, partnerships and joint ventures (A company's portion of the equity or loss generated by the affiliated entity should be debited, income, or credited, loss, to this account on a periodic basis. The offsetting entry should be debited or credited to 9100, income from partnerships, joint ventures, S-corporations, and limited liability corporations, provided that the investing company can exercise significant influence—usually more than 20% of the voting power—over the operations of the affiliated entity.)

**1750 Mortgage notes receivable, long-term**—Amounts of mortgages that are due after the next fiscal year end

**1760 Due from affiliated companies or subsidiaries, long-term**—Amounts due from affiliated companies or subsidiaries that are to be carried for a long period

**1780 Organization cost**—Legal fees, corporate charter fees, and other organization costs that are normally capitalized (Credit amortization of these fees directly to this account.)

### 1800-1890 Property, Plant, and Equipment

1810 **Land**—Cost of land acquired for the purpose of constructing company offices and warehouses and held for investment (Land held for future development should be included in 1320, land held for development.)

1820 **Buildings**—Costs relating to offices, warehouses, field offices, field warehouse, and other company structures used in the operation of the business

1825 **Rental property**—Cost of property owned and managed by the company and held for investment (Buildings used in the operation of the business should be classified in 1820, buildings.)

1827 **Recreation amenities**—Property the company retains for ownership and operation (Include property to be turned over to a home owners' association in 1430, direct construction cost.

1830 **Office furniture and equipment**—Cost of office furniture, fixtures, and small equipment used by administrative and office personnel

1840 **Vehicles**—Cost of automobiles and trucks owned by the business

1850 **Construction equipment**—The cost of all construction equipment, excluding licensed motor vehicles (Charge or debit small tools of nominal value to 1440, indirect construction cost, or 4560, small tools and supplies.)

1870 **Model home furnishings**—Cost of model home furniture and furnishings

1880 **Leasehold improvements**—Cost of improvements made to leased property

1890 **Computer equipment and software**—Cost of computer hardware and software (They may be segregated to improve tracking.)

### 1900-1999 Accumulated Depreciation

1920 **Accumulated depreciation, buildings**—Accumulated depreciation on assets carried in 1820, Buildings

1925 **Accumulated depreciation, rental properties**—Accumulated depreciation on rental properties carried in 1825, rental property

1927 **Accumulated depreciation, recreation amenities**—Accumulated depreciation on property carried in 1827, recreation amenities

1930 **Accumulated depreciation, office furniture and equipment**—Accumulated depreciation on assets carried in 1830, office furniture and equipment

1940 **Accumulated depreciation, vehicles**—Accumulated depreciation on assets carried in 1840, vehicles

1950 **Accumulated depreciation, construction equipment**—Accumulated depreciation on assets carried in 1850, construction equipment

1970 **Accumulated depreciation, model home furnishings**—Accumulated depreciation on assets carried in 1870, model home furnishings

1980 **Accumulated depreciation, leasehold improvements**—Accumulated depreciation on assets carried in 1880, Leasehold improvements

1990 **Accumulated depreciation, computer equipment and software**—Accumulated depreciation on assets carried in 1890, computer equipment and software

## 2000-2990 Liabilities and Owners' Equity

### 2000-2090 Deposits by Customers

2010 **Contract deposits**—Down payments, earnest money, and deposits on contracts (Transfer and credit the deposit to the appropriate account in the

3000–3400 series, Sales and Revenues, when the sale is closed, and debit 2010, contract deposits.)

**2030 Tenant security deposit**—Refundable tenant deposits held to secure proper care of unit

**2040 Advance rent collected**—Rent collected from tenants that relate to a future period. (When the rental income is earned, debit this account, and credit 3200, rental property income.)

### 2100–2190 Accounts Payable

**2110 Accounts payable, trade**—Amounts payable on open account to suppliers and trade contractors

**2120 Retentions payable**—Amounts withheld from trade contractors until final completion and approval of their work

**2190 Accounts payable, other**—Other short-term open accounts due to non-trade individuals or companies

### 2200–2290 Notes Payable

**2200 Line of credit payable**—Outstanding balance on revolving line of credit

**2220 Acquisitions and development loans payable**—Control account for all loans from lending institutions for acquisition and development costs (Detail accounts for each acquisition or development may be provided by using an additional sub-ledger or a two-digit subclass to the main account number.)

**2230 Construction loans payable**—Control account for all loans from lending institutions for construction financing (Detail accounts for each construction loan payable may be provided by using an additional sub-ledger or a two-digit subclass to the main account number.)

**2240 Current portion of long-term debt**—Portion of principal payments included in 2510, long-term notes payable, and 2530, mortgage notes payable, that are due on notes to be paid within one year

**2290 Notes payable, other**—Notes payable to banks, other financial institutions, and other individuals that are due within one year

### 2300–2490 Other Current Liabilities

**2310 Social Security and Medicare**—Accumulated Social Security (FICA) and Medicare taxes withheld from employee payroll (This account is also used to accrue the employer portion of these taxes.)

**2320 Federal payroll tax, withheld and accrued**—Accumulated federal taxes withheld from employee payroll and owed to the federal government

**2330 State and local payroll tax, withheld and accrued**—Accumulated state taxes withheld from employee payroll and owed to state government (Credit funds withheld from employee pay, and debit payments to the state income tax division. Also include disability and other state withholding taxes. For multiple states, cities, or other local government withholdings, you may set up a separate account, or use a two-digit sub-account.)

**2340 Other payroll withholdings**—Other accumulated amounts withheld from employee payroll, such as employees' share of health insurance costs (Credit funds withheld from employee payroll, and debit payments to the proper agencies.)

**2345 Union withholding and benefits payable**—Accumulated amounts withheld from employee payroll in accordance with a collective bargaining agreement

(This account can also be used to accrue employer liability for union benefits such as pension and welfare, training, health insurance, and other required benefits. To accrue benefits, credit this account and debit 4150, union benefits. Debit this account for payments to the union or appropriate fund.)

**2350 Sales and use taxes payable**—Credit amount of tax received from purchasers and debit payments to the taxing authority (Note that taxes paid on material used in construction are debited to 1430, direct construction cost, or 3830, building material.)

**2360 Real estate taxes payable**—Credit the company's liability for real estate taxes incurred to date, and debit payments to the taxing authority

**2370 Income taxes payable**—Credit for accrual of the company's current liability for federal and state income and franchise taxes and debit payments to the taxing authorities

**2390 Accrued interest payable**—Credit interest accrued and payable and debit payments

**2400 Accrued salaries and wages payable**—Control account for accrued salaries and wages (Credit accrued salaries and wages and debit payments made.)

**2410 Accrued commissions payable**—Commissions earned but not yet paid (Credit the amount of commission due and debit payments.)

**2411 Accrued pension and profit-sharing expenses**—Pension and profit-sharing earned but not yet paid (Credit amount due and debit payments.)

**2420 Workers' Compensation insurance payable**—Amounts withheld from payment to trade contractors for Workers' Compensation insurance but not yet paid (This account can also accrue the employers' liability for Workers' Compensation for their employees.)

**2425 Other accrued expenses**—The liability for expenses that have been incurred, but invoices have not yet been received, or the expense has not been paid, such as professional fees, bonuses, commissions, and vacations (Detailed accounts for other accrued expenses may be provided by using an additional sub-ledger or adding a two-digit subclass to the main account number.)

**2430 Deferred income**—Advance payments made by tenants or other sources for which income is not yet earned (Credit advance payments to this account. Debit the account when the revenue is earned, and credit the appropriate income account.)

**2440 Due to affiliated companies or subsidiaries**—Amounts currently due to affiliated or subsidiary companies

**2450 Due to officers, stockholders, owners, partners**—Amounts currently due to officers, stockholders, owners, and partners

**2480 Billings in excess of costs**—Usually used by remodelers, custom builders, and commercial builders to record charges that exceed estimated costs (sometimes referred to as overbilling), using the percentage of completion method of accounting

**2490 Other current liabilities**—Miscellaneous current liabilities not otherwise classified

### 2500–2890 Long-Term Liabilities

**2510 Long-term notes payable**—Control account for notes on vehicles, equipment, and other assets used in operations (Include current portion in 2240, current portion of long-term debt. Detailed accounts for long-term payable liabilities may be provided by using an additional sub-ledger or a two-digit subclass to the main account number.)

2530 **Mortgage notes payable**—Control account for mortgages on rental property and land and buildings used in operations (Include current portion in 2240, current portion of long-term debt. Detailed accounts for mortgage notes payable may be provided by using an additional sub-ledger or a two-digit subclass to the main account number.)

2600 **Deferred income taxes payable**—Income taxes due on deferred income

2610 **Due to affiliated companies or subsidiaries, long-term**—Amounts due to affiliated companies or subsidiaries that are to be carried for a long-term period.

2620 **Due to officers, stockholders, owners, partners, long-term**—Amounts due to company officers, stockholders, owners and partners to be carried for a long-term period

2700 **Other long-term liabilities**—Long-term liabilities not otherwise classified

### 2900–2990 Owners' Equity

2900 **Common stock**—Par value or stated value of stock outstanding

2910 **Additional paid in capital**—Amounts received in excess of par or stated value of stock

2920 **Retained earnings**—Prior years' accumulation of profits or losses

2930 **Treasury stock**—The corporation's own capital stock which has been issued and then reacquired by the corporation by either purchase or gift

2940 **Unrealized holding loss**—Represents cumulative unrealized loss on investments or marketable securities (Investments or marketable securities should be adjusted to the market value on an annual or periodic basis.)

2950 **Partnership or proprietorship account**—A separate account for each partner, indicating accumulated equity to date (Detailed accounts for partnership or proprietorship account may be provided by using an additional sub-ledger or adding a two-digit subclass to the main account number.)

2960 **Distributions, dividends, and draws**—Accumulated owners' withdrawals for period (Maintain a separate account for each owner. Debit distributions, dividends, and draws to this account. At the end of the fiscal year, close the account by crediting this account and debiting the amounts to 2920, retained earnings, or 2950, partnership or proprietorship account, as applicable. Detailed accounts for distributions, dividends, and draws may be provided by using an additional sub-ledger or adding a two-digit subclass to the main account number.)

## 3000–3990 Sales, Revenues, and Cost of Sales

### 3000–3490 Sales and Revenues

3000 **Sales, land held for development**—Revenues earned from sales of raw land not yet subdivided, and without improvements

3050 **Sales, developed lots**—Revenues earned from sales of partially or fully developed lots

3100 **Sales, single-family, speculative**—Revenues earned from sales of spec houses

3110 **Sales, single-family, production**—Revenues earned from sales of production houses

**3120 Sales, single-family, custom designed**—Revenues earned from sales of custom houses

**3125 Sales, single-family, custom, no land**—Revenues earned from sales of houses built under contract on land owned by someone other than the builder

**3130 Sales, residential remodeling**—Revenues earned from sales of residential remodeling work

**3133 Sales, commercial and industrial remodeling**—Revenues earned from sales of commercial and industrial remodeling work

**3135 Sales, insurance restoration**—Revenues earned from sales of insurance restoration work

**3137 Sales, repairs**—Revenues earned from sales of repair work

**3140 Sales, multifamily**—Revenues earned from sales of multifamily units

**3150 Sales, commercial and Industrial**—Revenues earned from sales of new commercial and industrial construction

**3160 Sales, trade-Ins, and repossessions**—Revenues earned from sales of houses originally received as partial payment on another sale or repossessions

**3190 Sales, other**—Revenues earned from sales of construction activities not otherwise classified

**3195 Cancellation fees**—Forfeiture of contract deposits

**3200 Rental property income**—Revenues earned from rental of investment property and office space

**3210 Common area reimbursements**—Revenues earned from tenant reimbursement of common area expenses (Common area expenses should be charged to the applicable account within the 7000 series. Other reimbursements should be credited to 3220, other reimbursements.)

**3220 Other reimbursements**—Revenues earned from tenant reimbursement of expenses (Expenses incurred by the company should be charged to the applicable account within the 7000 series.)

**3230 Parking fee income**—Revenue earned from the rental of company-owned parking facilities

**3240 Amenities facilities income**—Revenue earned from rental and use charges for company-owned recreational facilities

**3360 Construction management fee income**—Revenues earned from construction management activities

**3379 Design fees collected**—Revenues earned from design activities

**3400 Miscellaneous income**—Revenues earned from sources not otherwise classified

**3410 Interest income**—Interest earned from certificates of deposits, savings accounts, and other sources

**3420 Dividend income**—Dividends earned from investments in stocks, bonds, and other sources

**3450 Earned discounts**—Cash discounts earned from payment on account within the time established by the supplier or trade contractor

**3460 Earned rebates**—Incentives received from manufacturer for use of their products

**3490 Sales concessions and discounts**—Accumulates the difference between the published sales price and the contract price (This account captures the impact of concessions on company margins. If this account is used, the published price is placed in the appropriate sales account, and concessions and discounts are debited here. This contra account is a reduction to sales.)

### 3500–3700 Cost of Sales

**3500 Cost of sales, land held for development**—Includes transfers from 1320, land held for development, at the time of sale (Credit 1320 and debit 3500, cost of sales, land held for development.)

**3550 Cost of sales, developed lots**—Allocated amount to be written off on lots sold (Credit 1420, if the lot was developed prior to purchase, or 1412, accumulated allocations, land and land development costs, if the company developed the lot. Debit 3550, cost of sales, developed lots.)

**3600 Cost of sales, single-family, speculative**—Direct construction costs related to sales of homes recorded in 3100, sales, single-family, speculative (Transfer from and credit 1430, direct construction cost. Debit 3600.)

**3610 Cost of sales, single-family, production**—Direct construction costs of houses built under contract (Transfer from Account 1430, Direct construction cost. Debit 3610, cost of sales, single-family, production.)

**3620 Cost of sales, single-family, custom designed**—Direct construction costs of custom houses (Transfer from 1430, direct construction cost, if applicable. Debit 3620, cost of sales, single-family, custom designed.)

**3625 Cost of sales, single family, custom, no land**—Direct construction costs of custom homes built on land owned by someone other than the builder (Transfer from 1430, direct construction cost, if applicable. Debit 3625, cost of sales, single-family, custom, no land.)

**3630 Cost of sales, remodeling**—Direct construction costs of remodeling (Transfer from 1430, direct construction cost, if applicable. Debit 3630, cost of sales, remodeling. Alternatively, use the 3800 series to directly post remodeling costs to cost of sales.)

**3633 Cost of sales, commercial and industrial remodeling**—Direct construction costs of commercial and industrial jobs (Transfer from 1430, direct construction cost, if applicable. Debit 3633, cost of sales, commercial and industrial remodeling.)

**3635 Cost of sales, insurance restoration**—Direct costs for insurance restoration work (Transfer from 1430, direct construction cost, if applicable. Debit 3635, cost of sales, insurance restoration.)

**3637 Cost of sales, repairs**—Direct costs for repairs (Transfer from 1430, direct construction cost, if applicable. Debit 3637, cost of sales, repairs.)

**3640 Cost of sales, multifamily**—Direct construction costs of multifamily units sold (Transfer from 1430 direct construction cost. Debit 3640 cost of sales, multifamily.)

**3650 Cost of sales, commercial and industrial**—Direct construction costs of commercial and industrial jobs (Transfer from 1430, direct construction cost, if applicable. Debit 3650, cost of sales, commercial and industrial.)

**3660 Cost of sales, trade-ins**—Trade-in allowance and refurbishing (Transfer from 1530, trade-ins and repossessions, at the time of sale. Debit 3660, cost of sales, trade-ins.)

**3690 Cost of sales, other**—Costs incurred to generate income from sources not otherwise classified

3700 **Direct construction cost for prior periods**—Cost adjustments to cost of sales for charges or credits from prior period closings (These adjustments are for changes in cost that have not been accounted for after closing an individual unit.)

### 3800–3899 *Costs of Construction*

The following accounts can be used by remodelers and builders to directly post construction costs to cost of sales, instead of posting direct construction costs to 1430, direct construction cost.)

3810 **Direct labor**—Includes the gross wages paid to lead carpenters and crews engaged in the remodeling process

3820 **Labor burden**—Payroll taxes and Workers' Compensation insurance, as well as other items such as health insurance, life and disability insurance that relate to gross wages paid to the field crew (Also, includes vacation, holiday, sick days, and other paid days off for the field crew.)

3830 **Building material**—Cost of materials used on a remodeling project (Also includes all freight and taxes paid on the material in this account.)

3840 **Trade contractors**—Cost of trade contractors used on a specific remodeling project

3850 **Rental equipment**—Cost of rental equipment used on a specific remodeling project

3860 **Other direct construction costs**—Includes cost of small tools consumed on a specific remodeling project, cost of permits and fees for a particular project, and any other direct construction costs not otherwise classified

3870 **Professional design fees**—Costs paid to architects, engineers, interior designers, certified kitchen designers, and bath designers for use on a specific remodeling job (Also includes in-house design salaries, wages, and the related labor burden in this account if they are incurred on a specific remodeling job.)

## 4000–4990 Indirect Construction Cost

The 4000 series of accounts is an alternative to 1440, indirect construction cost. The 4000 series allows a detailed breakdown of accounts in the general ledger while maintaining a four-digit numerical code. The indirect costs accumulated in these accounts must still be allocated to houses or specific jobs held in inventory to comply with GAAP and IRS regulations.

### 4000–4090 *Salaries and Wages*

Salaries and wages of personnel directly engaged in the construction process, but not identified with a specific unit

4010 **Superintendents**—Salaries of supervisory personnel for time spent in organizing, planning, or supervising production crews (This category does not include wages of personnel who work on specific jobs and their crews.)

4020 **Laborers**—Wages paid to laborers on construction that cannot be charged to a specific job. (If possible, labor should be estimated, budgeted, and charged to a specific job.)

4030 **Production manager**—Salaries paid to the supervisors of superintendents

4040 **Architects, drafters, estimators, purchasers**—Salaries and wages of persons who perform these duties for construction jobs (If this function is a department unto itself, each person's job may be broken down into a separate account.)

4050 **Warranty and customer service manager**—Salaries of employees responsible for the warranty and service function

4060 **Warranty and customer service wages**—Labor incurred to repair, replace, or service any item on a particular unit after possession by owner

4070 **Other indirect construction wages**—Salaries and wages of personnel such as timekeepers, security guards, and quality control inspectors who are involved in the construction process but not identified with specific units

4990 **Absorbed indirect costs**—Used as a contra account to allocate the proportional share of indirect construction cost to work in process inventories to comply with IRS and GAAP requirements (This contra account requires a year-end closing adjustment, which is usually handled by an accountant.)

### 4100–4190 Payroll Taxes and Benefits

4110 **Payroll taxes**—The accumulated share of FICA, unemployment, Medicare, Social Security, and other company-paid taxes related to salaries and wages charged as indirect cost

4120 **Workers' Compensation insurance**—Insurance premiums for individual construction workers

4130 **Health and accident insurance**—Premiums for health and accident insurance for indirect construction workers

4140 **Retirement, pension, profit sharing**—Employer contributions to retirement, pension, and profit-sharing plans for indirect construction workers

4150 **Union benefits**—Benefits related to indirect construction workers in accordance with a collective bargaining agreement

4190 **Other benefits**—Benefits related to salaries and wages charged as indirect costs not otherwise classified

### 4200–4290 Field Office Expenses

Maintenance and repairs, utilities, telephone and other expenses incidental to a field office, including erection and moving. The field office is often a trailer; if the office is in model, include these expenses in the 6600 series of accounts (model home maintenance).

4210 **Rent, field office**—Rent for field office

4230 **Repairs and maintenance, field office**—Repairs and maintenance of field office, including service contracts

4250 **Utilities, field office**—Heat, electricity and other utilities for field office

4260 **Telephone, field office**—Installation and monthly charges for field office telephone and related communications equipment

4265 **Mobile phones, pagers, and radios, field office**—Purchase and monthly charges for cellular phones, pagers, and field radios for construction personnel

4290 **Other field office expenses**—Expenses for field office not included in other categories

### 4300–4390 Field Warehouse and Storage Expense

Costs incurred in material handling and storage if materials are not delivered to the jobsite by supplier

4310 **Rent, field warehouse and storage**—Rent on warehouse and storage facilities

4330 **Repairs and maintenance, field warehouse and storage**—Repairs and maintenance of warehouse and storage facilities, including service contracts

4350 **Utilities, field warehouse and storage**—Heat, electricity and other utilities for warehouse and storage facilities

4360 **Telephone, field warehouse and storage**—Installation and monthly charges for telephone in warehouse and storage

### 4400–4490 Construction Vehicles, Travel, and Entertainment

4410 **Lease payments, construction vehicles**—Payments on leased or rented vehicles used by construction personnel

4420 **Mileage reimbursement**—Payment to field personnel for use of their private vehicles

4430 **Repairs and maintenance, construction vehicles**—Repair and maintenance costs for automobiles and trucks used by construction personnel (Includes both minor and major work.)

4440 **Operating expenses, construction vehicles**—Fuel, oil, and lubrication expenses for automobiles and trucks used by construction personnel

4450 **Taxes, licenses, insurance, construction vehicles**—Property damage and liability insurance, licenses, fees, and taxes on vehicles used by construction personnel

4460 **Travel, construction department**—Travel expenses incurred by construction personnel

4470 **Customer business entertainment, construction**—Business-related entertainment expenses incurred by construction personnel

4480 **Training and education, construction**—Training and education expenses incurred by construction personnel

4490 **Recruiting fees and expenses, construction**—Expenses associated with the hiring of construction personnel

### 4500–4590 Construction Equipment

Costs of maintaining and operating construction equipment

4510 **Rent, construction equipment**—Payments on leased or rented equipment

4530 **Repairs and maintenance, construction equipment**—Repair and maintenance costs on equipment

4540 **Operating expenses, construction equipment**—Fuel, oil, and lubrication expenses on equipment

4550 **Taxes and insurance, construction equipment**—Taxes and insurance required on equipment

4560 **Small tools and supplies**—Cost of items such as hand tools, shovels, skill saws, small power tools, and extension cords, used in construction

### 4600–4690 Expenses for Maintaining Unsold Units and Units under Construction

Costs applicable to units under construction, prior to delivery to customer

4610 **Temporary utilities**—Utility hook-up costs and utility bills related to units under construction (Custom and small-volume builders may consider classifying these costs as part of direct construction cost.)

4620 **Trash maintenance**—Cost of trash hauling, dumpsters, and other equipment necessary for construction site maintenance

**4640 Lawn care**—Costs required to maintain the lawn prior to transfer to customer

**4650 Utilities, completed units**—Utility cost and hookups for finished units held in inventory and awaiting sale

**4660 Repairs and maintenance, completed units**—Cost of repair and maintenance to any unit held in inventory for sale

*4700–4790 Warranty and Customer Service*

**4710 Salaries and wages, warranty**—Labor incurred to repair, replace, or service any item after possession of a unit by owner

**4720 Material, warranty**—Price of materials to repair, replace, or service any item after possession of a unit by owner

**4730 Trade contractor, warranty**—Cost of trade contractor, incurred to repair, replace, or service any item after possession of a unit by owner

**4790 Other warranty expenses**—Costs—other than labor, materials, or trade contractors—incurred to repair, replace, or service any item after possession of a unit by owner

*4800–4890 Depreciation Expenses*

**4820 Depreciation, construction office**—Depreciation expense of construction office equipment

**4830 Depreciation, warehouse**—Depreciation expense of warehouse

**4840 Depreciation, construction vehicles**—Depreciation expense of construction vehicles

**4850 Depreciation, construction equipment**—Depreciation expense of construction equipment

*4900–4990 Other*

**4910 Insurance and bonding expenses**—Cost of obtaining insurance or bonding for construction projects and properties

**4920 Builder's risk insurance**—Cost of obtaining builder's risk insurance (Custom and small-volume builders may be more inclined to treat this as a direct cost.)

**4990 Absorbed indirect costs**—To comply with IRS and GAAP requirements and allocate the proportional share of indirect construction cost to work in process inventories (This contra account requires a year-end closing adjustment, which is usually handled by an accountant.)

# 5000–5990 Financing Expenses

*5000–5090 Interest*

**5010 Interest on line of credit**—Interest expense on loans held by banks and other lenders for operating capital

**5020 Interest on notes payable**—Interest expense on notes payable for fixed assets such as office buildings and vehicles

**5030 Interest expense on developed lots**—Interest expense on developed lots not currently under construction

**5040 Interest incurred on construction loans**—Interest expense paid during the building of a house (To comply with IRS and GAAP requirements, interest on construction loans must be capitalized during the construction period. If interest is posted to this account, allocate the proportionate share of interest to work-in-process inventories to comply with IRS and GAAP requirements at year end.)

5050  **Interest on completed speculative inventory**—Interest expense paid on completed speculative homes before closing on the units

5090  **Interest expense, other**—Other interest paid or accrued

### 5100–5190  *Construction Loan Points and Fees*

5120  **Points and fees**—Expenses paid on points and fees for construction loans

5130  **Appraisal and related fees**—Service charges paid for appraisal of property related to construction loans

5140  **Inspection fees**—Fees for inspection by lenders

### 5200–5290  *Closing Costs*

Closing costs related to the sale of finished houses

5210  **Closing costs**—Closing costs related to the sale of finished houses (including property and real estate taxes) paid by the seller (Custom and small-volume builders may charge closing costs as a direct expense. If they are paid on buyer's behalf as a concession, include in 6930, sales concessions.)

5220  **Title and recording**—Fees charged for searching and recording and for title insurance

5230  **Loan fees**—Origination or standby fees on permanent financing commitments

# 6000–6990  **Sales and Marketing Expenses**

This section of the operating expense chart of accounts is reserved for sales and marketing expenses that may be written off as period expenses.

### 6000–6090  *Sales Salaries, Commissions*

6010  **Compensation, sales manager**—Compensation, including bonuses or incentives, for sales managers

6030  **Salaries, sales personnel**—Salaries for noncommissioned activities, excluding draws against present or future commissions

6040  **Sales commissions, in-house**—Commissions paid to employees (Remodelers sometimes charge these commissions as a direct cost.)

6050  **Sales commissions, outside**—Commissions paid to sales agents and others not employed by the company

6090  **Other sales office salaries and wages**—Salaries and wages for clerical and other personnel who work directly for the sales department or sales office, including hostesses and sales assistants

### 6100–6190  *Payroll Taxes and Benefits, Sales and Marketing*

Payroll taxes and benefits associated with salaries and wages of the sales and marketing department or sales office employees

6110  **Payroll taxes, sales and marketing**—Accumulated share of FICA, unemployment, and other taxes relating to salaries and wages of sales and marketing personnel

6120  **Workers' compensation insurance, sales and marketing**—Insurance premiums on salaries and wages of sales and marketing personnel

6130  **Health and accident insurance, sales and marketing**—Premiums for health and accident insurance for sales and marketing personnel

**6140 Retirement, pension, profit-sharing plans, sales and marketing**—Employer contributions paid to retirement, pension, and profit-sharing plans for sales and marketing personnel

**6190 Other benefits, sales and marketing**—Benefits relating to salaries and wages of sales and marketing personnel

### *6200–6290 Sales Office Expenses*

Operating costs related to a separate sales office or design center. (If the sales office is in a model home, include expenses in the 6660–6690 series, model home maintenance.)

**6210 Rent, sales office**—Rental of sales office

**6230 Repairs and maintenance, sales office**—Cost of all interior and exterior sales office building repairs and maintenance, including interior remodeling not capitalized, janitorial service, landscaping, and window washing

**6250 Utilities, sales office**—Heat and other utilities for sales office

**6260 Telephone, sales office**—Installation and monthly charges, both land-line and cell phones for sales office

**6270 Supplies, sales office**—Office supplies used by sales office staff

### *6300–6395 Advertising and Sales Promotion*

**6310 Print advertising**—Classified and display advertising expenses

**6320 Radio advertising**—Expenses for radio time and related services

**6325 Television advertising**—Expenses for television time and related services

**6330 Internet fees, Web page design and maintenance expense**—Expenses for Internet fees, design of Web pages and related maintenance

**6340 Brochures and catalogs**—Cost of designing and printing brochures and catalogs

**6350 Signs**—Expenses for photography, typography, printing, artwork, copywriting, materials, and supplies required to make signs

**6355 Billboards**—Fees paid for art and advertising on billboards

**6365 Promotions**—Fees paid for special programs and items, such as move-in gifts

**6370 Agency commissions**—Fees paid to agencies that assist in setting up advertising programs

**6380 Multiple listing fees**—Payments to a centralized brokerage service

**6390 Public relations**—Fees paid to public relations firms for press releases and other publicity

**6395 Referral fees**—Payments for referrals

### *6400–6490 Sales Vehicles, Travel, and Entertainment*

**6410 Lease payments, sales vehicles**—Payments on leased or rented vehicles used for sales and marketing personnel

**6420 Mileage reimbursement**—Payment to sales and marketing personnel for use of their private vehicles

**6430 Repairs and maintenance, sales vehicles**—Repair and maintenance costs for the company's automobiles used by sales and marketing personnel, including both minor and major work

**6440 Operating expense, sales vehicles**—Fuel, oil, and lubrication costs

**6450 Taxes, licenses, insurance, sales vehicles**—Property damage and liability insurance, licenses, fees, and taxes on company vehicles used by sales and marketing personnel

**6460 Travel, sales and marketing**—Travel expenses incurred by sales and marketing personnel

**6470 Customer business entertainment**—Entertainment expenses incurred by sales and marketing personnel

### 6600–6690 Model Home Maintenance

**6610 Rent or lease payments, model home furnishings**—Costs of renting or leasing model home furnishings

**6620 Model home rent or lease payments**—Costs of renting or leasing the model home

**6625 Decorating fees, model home**—Fees for decorating services

**6630 Repairs and maintenance, model homes**—Repairs, maintenance, and decoration expenses resulting from use, damage, or minor changes to the model or its furnishings

**6650 Utilities, model homes**—Heat, electricity, water and sewer expenses

**6670 Lawn and landscaping care, model homes**—Labor and material costs for lawn maintenance, including mowing, watering, seeding or sodding, and fertilizing lawns and pruning other vegetation

**6680 Cleanup, model homes**—Costs relating to window washing and daily cleanup

**6690 Interest on model homes**—Interest paid after completion of the model home(s)

### 6700–6790 Sales and Marketing Fees

**6710 Market research and consultation**—Fees for market research and consultation

**6720 Interior design fee**—Fees paid for outside designers to assist buyers with their selections

**6770 Recruiting fees and expenses, sales and marketing personnel**—Expenses associated with the hiring of sales and marketing personnel

**6780 Training and education expenses**—Cost of travel and registration fees for seminars and conventions, meals and lodging expenses, in-house programs, literature, and materials (Also includes expenses incurred for conventions and trade shows, as well as national, state, and local association meetings.)

### 6800–6890 Depreciation

**6810 Depreciation, sales office**—Depreciation on sales office

**6830 Depreciation, sales vehicles**—Depreciation on sales and marketing vehicles

**6870 Depreciation, model home furnishings and decorations**—Depreciation on model home furnishings and decorations

### 6900–6990 Other Marketing Expenses

**6930 Sales concessions**—Announced discounts and other incentives (such as gifts and travel incentives) provided to customers as part of marketing and sales strategy

**6940 Buy downs**—Refunds of interest and points issued to customers during the sales process

**6999 Other sales and marketing expenses**—Sales and marketing expenses not otherwise classified

## 7000–7990 Operating and Management Expense, Rental Operations

*7000–7090 Property Management*

**7010 Compensation, property manager**—Compensation, including bonuses and incentives, for managers of property management personnel

**7030 Salaries and wages, property management personnel**—Direct salaries and wages for noncommission activities, excluding draws against present and future commissions, which should be debited to 7040, commissions, in-house, or 7050, commissions, outside.)

**7040 Commissions, in-house**—Commissions paid to property management personnel employed by the company for leasing of rental property

**7050 Commissions, outside**—Commissions paid to sales agents and others not employed by the company for leasing of rental property

**7060 Salaries and wages, maintenance personnel**—Wages and salaries of company personnel assigned to the maintenance and repair of rental property (To track the different types of work performed by maintenance personnel—such as janitorial service, landscaping, and repair—a builder may want to add a 1 or 2 digit suffix to this account number for each type of work performed. For example, this account could include 706001 and so on.)

**7070 Payroll taxes and benefits, rental operations**—Cost of the company's FICA, Medicare, and federal and state unemployment insurance for rental personnel

**7072 Workers' compensation insurance, rental**—Insurance premiums on salaries and wages of rental personnel

**7073 Health and accident insurance, rental**—Premiums for health and accident insurance for rental personnel

**7074 Retirement, pension, and profit-sharing plans, rental**—Employer contributions to retirement, pension, and profit-sharing plans for rental personnel

**7079 Other benefits, rental**—Salaries and wages for in-house clerical and other personnel involved in property management activities not otherwise classified

*7100–7190 Rental Expenses*

**7110 Advertising**—Advertising costs directly related to the renting of individual rental units

**7130 Credit reports**—Charges from credit bureaus for reports about prospective tenants

**7190 Other rental expenses**—Rental expenses not otherwise classified, such as concessions to tenants

*7200–7290 Administrative Expense, Rental Operations*

**7220 Management and service fees**—Fees paid to outside firms for the management and operation of a company-owned property management activity

**7230 Office expenses**—Costs of maintaining an office for a property management activity, including rent, supplies, and postage

**7240 Telephone**—Standard monthly charges and long distance costs directly related to a property management activity

**7250 Tenant bad debts**—Write-off of past-due rents receivable from tenants

**7260 Collection costs**—Costs incurred in pursuing collection of past-due rents receivable, including collection agency fees

**7290 Other administrative expenses**—Administrative expenses of a property management activity not otherwise classified

### 7300–7390 *Professional Services, Rental Operations*

7310 **Legal services**—Charges for legal counsel for all services relating to a property management activity

7320 **Accounting services**—Charges for preparation of financial statements, tax advice, and other services rendered by an outside accounting firm relating to a property management activity

7330 **Market research**—Charges from consulting firms or individuals for market research relating to a property management activity

7390 **Other professional services, rental operations**—Professional service costs for a property management activity not otherwise classified

### 7400–7490 *Operating Expense, Rental Operations*

7410 **Utilities**—Gas, electricity, water and sewer service, and other utilities for rental buildings

7420 **Engineering**—Payroll and other costs associated with engineering activities related to property management

7430 **Janitorial**—Costs for janitorial services for property management activity

7440 **Trash removal service**—Costs of contracted services for the removal of trash and other waste from related buildings

7450 **Exterminating**—Supplies and other costs associated with extermination services supplied by company personnel or an independent contractor

7460 **Snow removal**—Supplies and other costs associated with snow removal services supplied by company personnel or an independent contractor

7470 **Other contractual services**—Costs of services such as sign painting and design provided under contract for a property management activity and not otherwise classified

7480 **Vehicles and equipment, rental operations**—Cost of leasing and operating equipment for use at the rental property

7490 **Other rental operations expenses**—Operating costs of a rental property not otherwise classified

### 7500–7590 *Taxes and Insurance, Rental Operations*

7510 **Real estate property taxes**—Local taxes on rental property, land, improvements, and buildings

7520 **Personal property taxes**—Local taxes assessed on business-owned personal property at a rental property

7530 **Franchise taxes**—State tax on rental property for privilege of doing business

7540 **License fees**—Local fees for licenses, registrations, and permits

7560 **Workers' compensation insurance**—Costs for Workers' compensation insurance

7570 **Insurance, rental operations**—Costs for general liability, property damage, and extended fire insurance

7590 **Other taxes and insurance, rental operations**—Tax and insurance costs not otherwise classified

### 7600–7690 *Maintenance and Repair Expense, Rental Operations*

7610 **Tenant redecorating, rental operations**—Payroll, supplies, and all other costs associated with redecorating rental units; including services supplied by company personnel or independent contractors

7630  **Maintenance contracts and services, rental operations**—Charges from independent contractors for maintenance and repair services

7640  **Ground maintenance and repairs, rental operations**—Costs of maintaining rental property grounds, including landscaping provided by company personnel or independent contractors

7650  **Vehicle maintenance and repairs, rental operations**—Labor and material costs associated with the general maintenance and repair of company-owned vehicles used at a rental property

7660  **Equipment maintenance and repairs, rental operations**—Labor and materials costs incurred by company personnel or outside contractors for the maintenance and repair of equipment used at a rental property

7670  **Amenities maintenance and repairs, rental operations**—Labor and material costs incurred by company personnel or outside contractors for the maintenance and repair of recreational facilities at a rental property

*7700–7790  Financing Expenses, Rental Operations*
7710  **Interest on mortgage payable**—Interest charges associated with a permanent mortgage loan on rental buildings

7720  **Interest on long-term notes payable**—Interest charges from notes payable associated with rental operations

*7800–7890  Depreciation Expense, Rental Operations*
7810  **Depreciation, building**—Depreciation for buildings such as rental properties

7820  **Depreciation, maintenance equipment**—Depreciation for company-owned equipment used for maintaining rental premises

7830  **Depreciation, vehicles**—Depreciation for company-owned vehicles and maintenance equipment used at rental properties

7840  **Depreciation, furniture and fixtures**—Depreciation for company-owned furniture, fixtures, office machines, and office equipment used for rental operations

7850  **Depreciation, amenities**—Depreciation for rental property recreational facilities

7890  **Other depreciation**—Depreciation for assets used in rental operations not otherwise classified

*7900–7990  Other Management and Operating Expenses*
Management and operating expenses not otherwise classified

# 8000–8990  General and Administrative Expenses

*8000–8090  Salaries and Wages*
8010  **Salaries, owners**—Total compensation paid to owners, including salaries and bonuses

8020  **Salaries, officers**—Total compensation paid to nonowner company officers, including salaries and bonuses

8030  **Salaries, management**—Total compensation paid to upper- and middle-management personnel, other than owners or officers, including salaries and bonuses

8050  **Salaries and wages, office and clerical**—Total compensation paid to clerical and other personnel below the managerial level, including salaries, wages, and bonuses

**8090 Other general and administrative salaries and wages**—Total compensation paid to general and administrative personnel, and those not otherwise classified, including salaries, wages, and bonuses

### 8100–8190 Payroll Taxes and Benefits

**8110 Payroll taxes**—Cost of the company's FICA, Medicare, federal and state unemployment insurance, and other local taxes that relate to administrative salaries and wages

**8120 Workers' compensation insurance**—Insurance premiums for Workers' compensation, paid by the employer, for administrative and hourly employees

**8130 Health and accident insurance**—Health and accident insurance premiums, paid by the employer for administrative personnel

**8140 Retirement, pension, profit-sharing plans**—Employee contributions to retirement, pension, and profit-sharing plans for administrative personnel

**8190 Other employee benefits**—Benefits relating to salaries and wages of administrative personnel

### 8200–8290 Office Expenses

**8210 Rent**—Rental payments for administrative office space

**8220 Office equipment rental**—Rental payments on office equipment, cellular phones, and pagers for office personnel

**8230 Repairs and maintenance, administrative office space**—Costs of all interior and exterior administrative office building repairs and maintenance, including interior remodeling not capitalized, landscaping, janitorial service, and window washing

**8240 Repairs and maintenance, administrative office equipment**—All contracts and other charges for maintenance of office equipment

**8250 Utilities, administrative office**—Costs of utilities for the administrative offices

**8260 Telephone, administrative office**—Standard monthly fees and long-distance charges, including cell phones, not applied to other functions or departments

**8270 Office supplies, administrative office**—Printing, stationery, and other office supplies

**8280 Postage and deliveries**—Postage, express mail, couriers, FedEx, UPS, and other delivery services

**8290 Miscellaneous expenses, administrative office**—Office expenses not otherwise classified, including monthly answering service fees and paging services

### 8300–8390 Technology and Computer Expenses

**8310 Computer supplies**—Paper and all supplies necessary for the operation of the computer system

**8320 Leases, computer hardware**—Payments on leased hardware

**8330 Leases, computer software**—Payments on leased software

**8335 Software licensing and subscription fees**—Expenses associated with software licensing and subscription fees

**8340 Network and Web development expenses**—Costs related to intranet and extranet

**8350 Repairs and maintenance, computer equipment**—Service contract or other payments for the maintenance of computer hardware

**8360 Maintenance, computer software**—Contract or other payments for the maintenance agreement of the systems software

### 8400–8490 Vehicle, Travel, and Entertainment

8410  **Lease, administrative vehicles**—Payments on leased or rental vehicles used by administrative personnel

8420  **Mileage reimbursement**—Payments to administrative personnel for use of their private vehicles

8430  **Repairs and maintenance, administrative vehicles**—Repair and maintenance costs of automobiles used by administrative personnel, including both minor and major work

8440  **Operating expense, administrative vehicles**—Vehicle fuel, oil, and lubrication costs

8450  **Taxes, licenses, insurance, administrative vehicles**—Taxes, licenses, fees, and property damage and liability insurance on vehicles used by administrative personnel

8460  **Travel**—Travel expenses incurred by administrative personnel

8470  **Customer business expense**—Entertainment expenses incurred by administrative personnel

8480  **Meeting expenses**—Expenses incurred by officers and employees representing the company at various groups, industry meetings, and other external events

8490  **In-House meeting expenses**—Expenses incurred in holding in-house meetings

### 8500–8590 Taxes

8510  **Sales and use taxes**—Taxes imposed by the state, county, and city on non-direct construction cost materials used within the city limits but purchased outside those borders

8520  **Real estate taxes**—Tax on property used for the company's offices and realty taxes not charged elsewhere

8530  **Personal property taxes**—Assessment of personal property owned by the company

8540  **License fees**—License, registration, municipal fees, and operating permits

8590  **Other taxes**—Taxes not otherwise classified, such as state tax on capitalization and franchise tax

### 8600–8690 Insurance

8610  **Hazard insurance, property insurance**—Fire insurance and extended coverage on buildings and contents

8630  **General liability insurance**—Costs of liability insurance, including general and product liability insurance excluding vehicles

8690  **Other insurance**—Insurance premiums not otherwise classified

### 8700–8790 Professional Services

8710  **Accounting services**—Audit charges and charges for assistance in the preparation of financial statements, tax advice, and other services rendered by an outside accounting firm

8720  **Legal services**—Charges submitted by legal counsel for services rendered

8730  **Consulting services**—Service bureau, time-sharing, or professional fees for services rendered

8770 **Recruiting and hiring**—Expenses associated with hiring administrative personnel

8790 **Other professional expenses**—Professional fees not otherwise classified

### *8800–8890 Depreciation Expenses*

8810 **Depreciation, buildings**—Depreciation on company buildings such as administrative offices

8830 **Depreciation, vehicles**—Depreciation on company-owned vehicles used by administrative personnel

8840 **Depreciation, furniture, and equipment**—Depreciation on furniture, fixtures, office machines, and other equipment

8860 **Amortization of leasehold improvements**—Amortization of improvements to office buildings leased from another entity

8870 **Depreciation, computer equipment and software**—Deprecation for computer hardware and software programs (These items may be segregated for easier tracking and control.)

8880 **Amortization of organization cost**—Write-off of organization cost, including legal fees and corporate charter fees

8890 **Depreciation, other**—Depreciation and amortization charges not otherwise classified

### *8900–8990 General and Administrative Expense, Other*

8900 **Bad debts**—Charges for uncollectible receivables (Credit 1280, allowance for doubtful accounts.)

8905 **Legal settlement expenses**—Expenses dictated by the court as a result of legal action

8910 **Contributions**—All charitable donations

8911 **Contributions, political**—All contributions made to political organizations and candidates (These contributions are generally not deductible.)

8920 **Dues and subscriptions**—Trade association dues and subscriptions for magazines, newspapers, trade journals, business publications, reports, and manuals

8950 **Bank charges**—Bank fees for miscellaneous charges. (Check printing should be charged to 8270, office supplies, administrative office.)

8960 **Penalties and other nondeductible expenses**—Tax penalties, fines, parking tickets

8990 **Training and education expenses**—Cost of travel and registration fees for seminars and conventions, meals and lodging expenses, in-house programs, literature, and materials (Also includes expenses incurred for conventions and trade shows, as well as national, state, and local association meetings.)

# 9000–9990 Other Income and Expenses

### *9100–9190 Other Income*

Income derived from sources other than the primary activity of the business

9100 **Income from partnerships, joint ventures, S corporations (S corps), and limited liability corporations (LLCs)**—Income (loss) from participation in partnerships, joint ventures, S corps, and LLCs

9120 **Loss from impairment write-downs of developed lots**—Unrealized loss, created by the write-down of developed lots to reflect the lower of cost or market

**9150 Gain or loss on sale of assets**—Gain or loss (debit) on the sale of assets that had been used in the operation of the business, such as vehicles, computers, and office equipment

**9190 Other**—Income derived from sources other than the main activity of the business, including speaking and consulting fees, expert witness fees, home inspections, real estate commissions, and budgeting fees

*9200–9290 Other expenses*

Extraordinary expenses or expenses attributable to activities not related to the main activity of the business

**9200 Extraordinary expenses**—Expenses attributable to activities not related to the main activity of the business (Separate account numbers within this series can be set up to track different categories of other expenses.)

*9300–9390 Provision for Income Taxes*

Provision for federal and state taxes on current income

**9300 Provision for federal income taxes**

**9320 Provision for state income taxes**

**9330 Provision for local income taxes**

# Basic Accounts for Small-Volume Businesses

The following abbreviated list of accounts provides an example of the accounts typically used by small-volume builders constructing fewer than 25 units per year. Small-volume remodelers and developers can also adapt this group of basic accounts to their businesses. The complete NAHB Chart of Accounts, shown in Appendixes A and B, contains more accounts than are normally required to perform the accounting function of a small construction firm. Small-volume builders may use this list as a guide to establish their own chart of accounts: these numerical codes and accounting categories are compatible with those used in the complete NAHB Chart of Accounts.

## 1000–1990 Assets

### 1000–1090 Cash
    1010  Petty cash
    1020  Cash on deposit, general
    1040  Cash on deposit, savings and money market
    1050  Cash on deposit, held in escrow

### 1100–1190 Short-Term Investments
    1110  Certificates of deposit

### 1200–1290 Receivables
    1210  Accounts receivable, trade
    1230  Notes receivable

### 1400–1490 Construction Work in Progress
    1420  Developed lots
    1430  Direct construction cost
    1440  Indirect construction cost

#### 1600–1690 Other Current Assets
1610 Refundable deposits
1630 Employee advances
1660 Due from officers, stockholders, owners, or partners
1690 Other current assets

#### 1700–1790 Investments and Other Assets
1780 Organization cost

#### 1800–1890 Property, Plant, and Equipment
1830 Office furniture and equipment
1840 Vehicles
1850 Construction equipment
1880 Leasehold improvements
1890 Computer equipment and software

#### 1900–1990 Accumulated Depreciation
1930 Accumulated depreciation, office furniture and equipment
1940 Accumulated depreciation, vehicles
1950 Accumulated depreciation, construction equipment
1980 Accumulated depreciation, leasehold improvements
1990 Accumulated depreciation, computer equipment and software

## 2000–2990 Liabilities and Owners' Equity

#### 2000–2090 Deposits by Customers
2010 Contract deposits

#### 2100–2290 Accounts and Notes Payable
2110 Accounts payable, trade
2200 Line of credit payable
2230 Construction loans payable
2290 Notes payable, other

#### 2300–2490 Other Current Liabilities
2310 Social Security and Medicare
2320 Federal payroll tax, withheld and accrued
2330 State payroll tax, withheld and accrued
2340 Other payroll withholdings
2420 Workers' compensation insurance payable
2450 Due to officers, stockholders, owners, partners
2490 Other current liabilities

#### 2500–2890 Long-Term Liabilities
2510 Long-term notes payable
2530 Mortgage notes payable
2620 Due to officers, stockholders, owners, partners, long-term
2700 Other long-term liabilities

*2900–2990 Owners' Equity*
  2900  Common Stock
  2920  Retained Earnings
  2950  Partnership or proprietorship account
  2960  Distributions, dividends, and draws

# 3000–3990 Sales, Revenues, and Cost of Sales

*3000–3490 Sales and Revenues*
  3050  Sales, developed lots
  3110  Sales, single-family, production
  3120  Sales, single-family, custom designed
  3125  Sales, single–family, custom, no land
  3190  Sales, other
  3370  Design fees collected
  3400  Miscellaneous income
  3410  Interest income
  3420  Dividend income
  3450  Earned discounts

*3500–3790 Cost of Sales*
  3550  Cost of sales, developed lots
  3610  Cost of sales, single-family, production
  3620  Cost of sales, single-family, custom designed
  3625  Cost of sales, single-family, custom, no land
  3690  Cost of sales, other
  3700  Direct construction cost for prior periods

# 4000–4990 Indirect Construction Cost

  4010  Superintendents and construction supervision salaries and wages
  4120  Workers' compensation insurance
  4265  Mobile phones, pagers, radios, field office
  4410  Lease payments, construction vehicles
  4420  Mileage reimbursement
  4430  Repairs and maintenance, construction vehicles
  4440  Operating expenses, construction vehicles
  4450  Taxes, licenses, insurance, construction vehicles
  4510  Rent, construction equipment
  4530  Repairs and maintenance, construction equipment
  4540  Operating expenses, construction equipment
  4550  Taxes and insurance, construction equipment
  4560  Small tools and supplies
  4610  Temporary utilities
  4620  Trash maintenance
  4710  Salaries and wages, warranty
  4720  Material, warranty
  4920  Builder's risk insurance
  4990  Absorbed indirect costs

# 5000–5990  Financing Expenses

    5020  Interest on notes payable
    5040  Interest incurred on construction loans
    5090  Interest expense, other
    5120  Points and fees
    5210  Closing costs

# 6000–6990  Sales and Marketing Expenses

    6040  Sales commissions, in-house
    6050  Sales commissions, outside
    6310  Print advertising
    6330  Internet fees, Web page design and maintenance expense
    6340  Brochures and catalogs
    6350  Signs
    6365  Promotions
    6370  Agency commissions
    6395  Referral fees

# 8000–8990  General and Administrative Expense

    8010  Salaries, owners
    8050  Salaries and wages, office and clerical
    8110  Payroll taxes
    8120  Workers' compensation insurance
    8130  Health and accident insurance
    8140  Retirement, pension, profit-sharing plans
    8190  Other employee benefits
    8210  Rent
    8220  Office equipment rental
    8230  Repairs and maintenance, administrative office space
    8240  Repairs and maintenance, administrative office equipment
    8250  Utilities, administrative office
    8260  Telephone, administrative office
    8270  Office supplies, administrative office
    8280  Postage and deliveries
    8290  Miscellaneous expenses, administrative office
    8320  Leases, computer hardware
    8330  Leases, computer software
    8335  Software licensing and subscription fees
    8350  Repairs and maintenance, computer equipment
    8410  Lease, administrative vehicles
    8420  Mileage reimbursement
    8430  Repairs and maintenance, administrative vehicles
    8440  Operating expense, administrative vehicles
    8450  Taxes, licenses, insurance, administrative vehicles
    8460  Travel
    8470  Customer business expense

8520   Real estate taxes
8540   License fees
8590   Other taxes
8630   General liability insurance
8690   Other insurance
8710   Accounting services
8720   Legal services
8730   Consulting services
8770   Recruiting and hiring
8830   Depreciation, vehicles
8840   Depreciation, furniture and equipment
8860   Amortization of leasehold improvements
8870   Depreciation computer equipment and software
8880   Amortization of organization cost
8910   Contributions
8911   Contributions, political
8920   Dues and subscriptions
8950   Bank charges
8960   Penalties and other nondeductible expenses
8990   Training and education expenses

## 9000–9990  Other Income and Expenses

9150   Gain or loss on sale of assets
9190   Other
9200   Extraordinary expenses

# APPENDIX D

# Basic Accounts for Remodelers

The following abbreviated list of accounts provides an example of the accounts typically used by remodelers. The complete NAHB Chart of Accounts, shown in Appendices A and B, contains more accounts than are normally required to perform the accounting function of a small construction firm. Remodelers may use this list as a guide to establish their own chart of accounts: these numerical codes and accounting categories are compatible with those used in the complete NAHB Chart of Accounts.

## 1000~1990 Assets

1010  Petty cash
1020  Cash on deposit, general
1030  Cash on deposit, payroll
1040  Cash on deposit, savings and money market
1210  Accounts receivable, trade
1230  Notes receivable
1280  Allowance for doubtful accounts
1290  Retentions (retainage) receivable
1310  Construction materials inventory
1330  Property held for remodeling
1610  Refundable deposits
1620  Prepaid expenses
1630  Employee advances
1650  Due from affiliates or subsidiaries
1660  Due from officers, stockholders, owners, or partners
1690  Other current assets
1780  Organization cost
1810  Land
1820  Buildings
1830  Office furniture and equipment
1840  Vehicles

1850  Construction equipment
1880  Leasehold improvements
1890  Computer equipment and software

## 1900–1990  Accumulated Depreciation

1920  Accumulated depreciation, buildings
1930  Accumulated depreciation, office furniture and equipment
1940  Accumulated depreciation, vehicles
1950  Accumulated depreciation, construction equipment
1980  Accumulated depreciation, leasehold improvements
1990  Accumulated depreciation, computer equipment and software

## 2000–2990  Liabilities and Owners' Equity

2010  Contract deposits
2110  Accounts payable, trade
2120  Retentions payable
2200  Line of credit payable
2240  Current portion of long-term debt
2290  Notes payable, other
2310  Social Security and Medicare
2320  Federal payroll tax, withheld and accrued
2330  State payroll tax, withheld and accrued
2410  Accrued commissions payable
2420  Workers' compensation insurance payable
2425  Other accrued expenses
2440  Due to affiliated companies or subsidiaries
2450  Due to officers, stockholders, owners, or partners
2480  Billings in excess of costs
2490  Other current liabilities
2510  Long-term notes payable
2530  Mortgage notes payable
2700  Other long-term liabilities
2900  Common stock
2950  Partnership or proprietorship account
2920  Retained earnings
2960  Distributions, dividends, and draws

## 3000–3990  Sales, Revenues, and Cost of Sales

### 3000–3490  *Sales and Revenues*

3130  Sales, residential remodeling
3133  Sales, commercial and industrial remodeling
3135  Sales, insurance restoration
3137  Sales, repairs
3190  Sales, other
3370  Design fees collected
3400  Miscellaneous income

3410 Interest income
3420 Dividend income
3450 Earned discounts
3460 Earned rebates

### 3800–3899 Costs of Construction—Remodeling
3810 Direct labor
3820 Labor burden
3830 Building material
3840 Trade contractors
3850 Rental equipment
3860 Other direct construction costs
3870 Professional design fees

### 4000–4990 Indirect Construction Cost
4010 Superintendents
4020 Laborers
4030 Production manager
4040 Architects, drafters, estimators, purchasers
4110 Payroll taxes
4120 Workers' compensation insurance
4130 Health and accident insurance
4265 Mobile phones, pagers, radios, field
4410 Lease payments, construction vehicles
4420 Mileage reimbursement
4430 Repairs and maintenance, construction vehicles
4440 Operating expenses, construction vehicles
4450 Taxes, licenses, insurance, construction vehicles
4510 Rent, construction equipment
4530 Repairs and maintenance, construction equipment
4540 Operating expenses, construction equipment
4550 Taxes and insurance, construction equipment
4560 Small tools and supplies
4710 Salaries and wages, warranty
4720 Material, warranty
4730 Trade contractor, warranty

### 5000–5990 Financing Expenses
5010 Interest on line of credit
5020 Interest on notes payable
5090 Interest expense, other

### 6000–6990 Sales and Marketing Expenses
6030 Salaries, sales personnel
6040 Sales commissions, in-house
6050 Sales commissions, outside
6110 Payroll taxes, sales and marketing
6120 Workers' compensation insurance, sales and marketing
6130 Health and accident insurance, sales and marketing

6310  Print advertising
6330  Internet fees, Web page design and maintenance expenses
6340  Brochures and catalogues
6350  Signs
6390  Public relations
6395  Referral fees

### 8000–8990 General and Administrative Expense

8010  Salaries, owners
8050  Salaries and wages, office and clerical
8110  Payroll taxes
8120  Workers' compensation insurance
8130  Health and accident insurance
8140  Retirement, pension, profit-sharing plans
8210  Rent
8220  Office equipment rental
8230  Repairs and maintenance, administrative office space
8240  Repairs and maintenance, administrative office equipment
8250  Utilities, administrative office
8260  Telephone, administrative office
8270  Office supplies, administrative office
8280  Postage and deliveries
8320  Leases, computer hardware
8330  Leases, computer software
8335  Software licensing and subscription fees
8340  Network and web development expenses
8350  Repairs and maintenance, computer equipment
8410  Lease, administrative vehicles
8420  Mileage reimbursement
8430  Repairs and maintenance, administrative vehicles
8440  Operating expense, administrative vehicles
8450  Taxes, licenses, insurance, administrative vehicles
8460  Travel
8470  Customer business expense
8480  Meeting expenses
8530  Personal property taxes
8540  License fees
8590  Other taxes
8610  Hazard insurance, property insurance
8630  General liability insurance
8690  Other insurance
8710  Accounting services
8720  Legal services
8730  Consulting services
8770  Recruiting and hiring
8810  Depreciation, buildings
8830  Depreciation, vehicles
8840  Depreciation, furniture and equipment
8860  Amortization of leasehold improvements

8870 Depreciation, computer equipment and software
8880 Amortization of organization cost
8900 Bad debts
8910 Contributions
8911 Contributions, political
8920 Dues and subscriptions
8950 Bank charges
8960 Penalties and other nondeductible expenses
8990 Training and education expenses

## 9000–9990 Other Income and Expenses

### 9100–9190 Other Income
9150 Gain or loss on sale of assets
9190 Other

### 9200–9290 Other Expenses
9200 Extraordinary Expenses

# Direct Construction Costs, Subsidiary Ledger

## General Ledger Account 1430

*1000–1999 Preparation Preliminaries*
- 1010 Building permits
- 1020 HBA assessments
- 1030 Warranty fees
- 1110 Blueprints
- 1120 Surveys
- 1210 Lot clearing
- 1220 Fill dirt and material
- 1300 Demolition
- 1400 Temporary electric
- 1420 Individual wells
- 1430 Water service
- 1440 Septic system
- 1450 Sewer system
- 1460 Gas service
- 1470 Electric service
- 1480 Telephone service
- 1490 Other utility connections

*2000–2999 Excavation and Foundation*
- 2000 Excavation and backfill
- 2010 Plumbing—ground
- 2100 Footings and foundation
- 2105 Rebar and reinforcing steel
- 2110 Concrete block
- 2120 Rough grading
- 2130 Window wells
- 2200 Waterproofing
- 2300 Termite protection

### 3000–3999 Rough Structure

3100 Structural steel

3110 Lumber—1st package
3120 Lumber—2nd package
3130 Lumber—3rd package
3140 Trusses
3150 Miscellaneous lumber
3210 Framing labor—draw #1
3220 Framing labor—draw #2
3230 Framing labor—draw #3
3300 Windows
3350 Skylights
3400 Exterior siding
3410 Exterior trim labor
3500 Flatwork material
3550 Flatwork labor
3610 HVAC—rough
3720 Plumbing—rough
3810 Electrical—rough
3910 Gutters and downspouts

### 4000–4999 Full Enclosure

4100 Roofing material
4150 Roofing labor
4200 Masonry material
4250 Masonry labor
4300 Exterior doors
4350 Garage door
4400 Insulation
4500 Fireplaces
4600 Painting—exterior

### 5000–5999 Finishing Trades

5100 Drywall
5200 Interior trim material
5250 Interior trim labor
5300 Painting—interior
5400 Cabinets and vanities
5450 Countertops
5510 Ceramic tile
5520 Special flooring
5530 Vinyl
5540 Carpet
5610 Hardware
5620 Shower doors and mirrors
5630 Appliances
5700 HVAC—final
5710 Plumbing—final

5720 Electrical fixtures
5730 Electrical—final
5810 Wall coverings
5890 Special finishes

### 6000–6999 Completion and Inspection

6100 Clean-up
6200 Final grade
6300 Driveways
6400 Patios, walks
6450 Decks
6490 Fences
6500 Ornamental iron
6600 Landscaping
6700 Pools

# APPENDIX F

# Indirect Construction Costs, Subsidiary Ledger

## General Ledger Account 1440

### 4000–4090 Salaries and Wages
4010 Superintendents
4020 Laborers
4030 Production manager
4040 Architects, drafters, estimators, purchasers
4050 Warranty and customer service manager
4060 Warranty and customer service wages
4070 Other indirect construction wages

### 4100–4190 Payroll Taxes and Benefits
4110 Payroll taxes
4120 Workers' compensation insurance
4130 Health and accident insurance
4140 Retirement, pension, profit sharing
4150 Union benefits
4190 Other benefits

### 4200–4290 Field Office Expenses
4210 Rent, field office
4230 Repairs and maintenance, field office
4250 Utilities, field office
4260 Telephone, field office
4265 Mobile phones, pagers, radios, field office
4290 Other field office expenses

### 4300–4390 Field Warehouse and Storage Expenses
4310 Rent, field warehouse and storage
4330 Repairs and maintenance, field warehouse and storage

4350  Utilities, field warehouse and storage

4360  Telephone, field warehouse and storage

### 4400–4490  Construction Vehicles, Travel, and Entertainment

4410  Lease payments, construction vehicles

4420  Mileage reimbursement

4430  Repairs and maintenance, construction vehicles

4440  Operating expenses, construction vehicles

4450  Taxes, licenses, insurance, construction vehicles

4460  Travel, construction department

4470  Customer business entertainment, construction

4480  Training and education, construction

4490  Recruiting fees and expenses, construction

### 4500–4590  Construction Equipment

4510  Rent, construction equipment

4530  Repairs and maintenance, construction equipment

4540  Operating expenses, construction equipment

4550  Taxes and insurance, construction equipment

4560  Small tools and supplies

### 4600–4690  Expenses for Maintaining Unsold Units and Units Under Construction

4610  Temporary utilities

4620  Trash maintenance

4640  Lawn care

4650  Utilities, completed units

4660  Repairs and maintenance, completed units

### 4700–4790  Warranty and Customer Service

4710  Salaries and wages, warranty

4720  Material, warranty

4730  Trade contractor, warranty

4790  Other, warranty expenses

### 4800–4890  Depreciation Expenses

4820  Depreciation, construction office

4830  Depreciation, warehouse

4840  Depreciation, construction vehicles

4850  Depreciation, construction equipment

### 4900–4990  Other

4910  Insurance and bonding expenses

4920  Builder's risk insurance

4990  Absorbed indirect costs

# Land Development Costs, Subsidiary Ledger

## General Ledger Account 1410

*0100 Pre-Acquisition Costs*
   0101 Options
   0102 Fees
   0103 Professional services

*0110 Acquisition Costs*
   0111 Purchase price, undeveloped land
   0112 Sales commissions
   0113 Legal fees
   0114 Appraisals
   0115 Closing costs
   0116 Interest and financial fees

*0120 Land Planning and Design*
   0121 Bonds
   0122 Fees
   0123 Permits
   0124 Legal expenses
   0125 Land planner fee
   0126 Preliminary architecture
   0127 Landscape architecture
   0128 Marketing expenses
   0129 Property tax

*0130 Engineering*
   0131 Civil engineering
   0132 Soil testing
   0133 Environmental engineering
   0134 Traffic engineering
   0138 Project management

### 0140 Earthwork
0141 Fill dirt
0142 Clearing lot
0143 Rock removal
0144 Erosion control
0145 Dust control

### 0150 Utilities
0151 Sewer lines
0152 Storm sewer
0153 Water lines
0154 Gas lines
0155 Electric lines
0156 Telephone lines
0157 Cable television lines
0158 Special technology lines

### 0160 Streets and Walks
0161 Curbs and gutters
0162 Walkways
0163 Paving
0164 Street lights
0165 Street signs

### 0170 Signage
0171 Temporary
0172 Entry sign
0173 Permanent signs
0174 Street signs

### 0180 Landscaping
0181 Sod or seed
0182 Shrubs
0183 Trees
0184 Mulch
0185 Other materials
0186 Labor

### 0190 Amenities
0191 Recreation center
0192 Recreation center furnishings
0193 Exercise equipment
0194 Swimming pool
0195 Tennis court
0196 Tot lots
0197 Putting greens
0198 Exercise trail

# Glossary

**A**

**absorption costing.** One of two methods of accumulating cost in an accounting system (It requires including both direct and indirect costs in the total cost of each unit of production. Absorption costing combines the proportional share of indirect construction cost for the unit, job, or lot with its direct construction cost to determine the total cost of the unit, job, or lot.)

**accounting.** The process of collecting, classifying, and accumulating historical financial transactions in categories and reports that will accurately reflect operational performance (income statement) and the present financial position (balance sheet)

**accounting system.** Accumulates and summarizes financial data to generate the income statement, the balance sheet, and other reports

**accounts payable subsidiary.** Shows amounts currently owed to *each* supplier, trade contractor, and others

**acid test ratio.** A refinement of the current ratio (It uses only "quick assets," cash or any other current asset that easily can be converted to cash within 30 days, such as accounts receivables and short-term cash investments (Calculation of this ratio does not include inventories.)

**AICPA.** American Institute of Certified Public Accountants (It is the national professional organization for certified public accountants [CPAs] in the United States.)

**American Institute of Certified Public Accountants (AICPA).** The national professional organization for certified public accountants (CPAs) in the United States

**asset turnover ratio.** Measures how efficiently the company uses its resources (assets)

**assets.** Items of value that the company owns, either tangible or intangible (Tangible assets include cash; inventories [land, work in progress, and materials]; finished units; office furniture and equipment; and construction equipment and vehicles. Intangible assets lack physical substance and include organization costs, goodwill, and copyrights.)

# B

**balance sheet.** A snapshot of the financial position of a business as of the date on the statement (It includes assets and who has claims to them. Builders, remodelers, and developers use it to evaluate a company's financial strength, liquidity, and leverage.)

**breakeven point.** The number of units, jobs, or lots the company needs to sell to cover all costs and expenses (It results from dividing the contribution margin into the fixed cost.)

**breakeven analysis.** Establishes the sales volume needed to cover fixed expenses and when company's efforts begin to produce profits

# C

**capitalization.** The process of recording expenditures benefiting more than one time period as assets to be expensed proportionally over the period of benefit

**cash flow statement.** Analyzes the changes in cash during a given time period

**certified public accountant (CPA).** A professional designation with high educational and ethical requirements

**completed-contract method of recognizing revenue.** Recognizes revenue only when the contract is complete

**contribution margin.** The revenues minus the total variable cost and expenses (For a multiple-community project, contribution margin includes revenues, costs, and expenses that relate only to that specific community. It also goes to cover other company expenses not specific to any one community and contributes to the overall profit of the company. It is sometimes also referred to as *operating profit per community*.)

**conversion rates.** Traffic units divided by net contracts

**cost.** Associated with the creation of value and the manufacturing process (Cost is considered a business asset until the manufactured product, such as a new home, is sold. It is an item of value that a business owns prior to a sale. Costs that create value include the materials and labor used in each house plus the proportional cost associated with the construction process, indirect construction cost.)

**cost-benefit analysis.** Analysis to determine if a given cost will provide benefits above the cost

**cost of sales.** Costs associated with the products your business sells (For a builder, they would be lot cost and direct cost.)

**cost variance reports.** Show variances by reason, vendor, job, and other criteria of value to your company

**costing.** Allocating construction costs to units of production, such as finished lots, houses, or remodeling jobs

**CPA.** Certified public accountant

**current assets.** Cash and all other assets that could be converted into cash within a fiscal or calendar year (12 months)

**current liabilities.** Obligations to be paid within a 12-month period

# D

**direct construction costs.** Costs that builders, remodelers, and developers can trace to a specific unit of production: the cost of lumber, bricks, paint, and kitchen appliances (for builders and remodelers); materials, such as asphalt for roads (for developers); and the cost of labor hours for the trades such as excavators, framers, roofers, and masons

**direct costing.** One of two methods of accumulating cost in an accounting system (It includes only direct construction cost—direct material and direct labor—to each unit of production.)

# E

**equities.** The source of capital (either from the owners, creditors, or lenders) used to acquire assets (They are claims to the assets of a business by creditors, lenders, owners, and investors.)

**expense.** Relates to day-to-day business operations (Accountants sometimes refer to expenses as *period costs* because they often relate to the passage of time. Examples of such expenses include rent, insurance, telephone, advertising, interest, and commissions.)

# F

**Financial Accounting Standards Board (FASB).** Authorizes and makes the accounting rules of the United States under the auspices of the U.S. Securities and Exchange Commission

**financial analysis.** An analytical review of the financial information accumulated in the accounting system and reported in the financial statements (It helps identify trends and compare the data in the financial reports with predetermined goals, industry standards, and data from prior periods.)

**financing expenses.** The cost of borrowing money from financial institutions or other third-party sources, including interest, points, and fees paid in relation to borrowing or commitments to borrow money (They include development and construction loans, commitments for permanent financing, points, other fees paid at closings, and funds borrowed for operating capital.)

**financial ratios.** Measure liquidity, profitability, financial strength, efficiencies, leverage, and return on investment (They also identify relationships among the different classifications in financial statements, financial strength, efficiency of operation, return on investment, and other factors.)

**fixed costs and expenses.** Remain constant within a volume range (They do not change with the number of homes built within a set volume range. They typically include personnel costs, leases on space and equipment, and office costs.)

# G

**general and administrative expenses.** Expenses that are associated with a specific time period rather than to a particular home, lot, or job (They are charged against revenues received during the same time period and include administrative salaries, financing, sales and marketing, office rent, telephone service, office supplies, books and subscriptions, insurance, licenses, travel and entertainment, educational programs, and professional fees.)

**general ledger.** Shows all financial transactions summarized by account

**gross profit margin.** What the company has left from the sale after paying for land and construction costs

**gross profit ratio.** The result of dividing sales into gross profit

**gross profit report.** A report of every house closed during the reporting period that provides a quick preview of the profitability of each one

## H

**holding power.** Refers to how long the company would be able to stay in business during a downturn or when sales are not occurring at the anticipated velocity

## I

**income statement.** A profit and loss statement that summarizes the results of financial transactions occurring during a particular time period—a month, a quarter, six months, or a year (It covers all revenue sources, costs, and expenses associated with the period.)

**indirect construction costs.** The expenses to run the construction department (These costs incurred in the construction process do not become part of the homes. Examples of indirect construction costs include the salaries of the superintendents and the cost of the field office, trucks, telephones, and electronic devices. When using absorption costing they are allocated proportionally to each house or unit of production. When using direct costing, they are also called *period costs* because they are charged against revenues in the period in which they are incurred.)

**internal control system.** Protects a company's assets including cash inventories, equipment, and the like; ensures that accounting records are accurate and reliable; promotes operational efficiency; and encourages employees to follow established policies and procedures

**inventory turnover ratio.** Results from dividing the dollar value of inventory into sales (This ratio allows a builder or developer to evaluate field efficiencies and inventory levels. It reflects construction efficiency and cycle time.)

## J

**journalizing.** The first step in processing financial data (The bookkeeper enters daily data in chronological order in journals as he or she receives information on financial transactions.)

## L

**ledgers.** Summarize financial transactions by account (Debits and credits to the accounts are posted in the general ledger and subsidiary ledgers from the *journals* or books of original entry.)

**leverage.** Involves using credit to support a business's or owner's financial standing (It uses borrowed assets from third parties or resources provided by outsiders to increase the return on the owners' investment.)

**leverage factor.** Refers to how much third-party financing the owner is using to run the company compared with owner's capital (The more third-party financing used, the higher the leverage factor and as a consequence the higher the risk.)

**liabilities.** Obligations the company owes to third parties, such as accounts payable, construction loan payments, other loans payable, and taxes (They are claims of creditors and lenders.)

**liquidity.** Solvency, the ability to convert assets to cash, or the ability to pay current debts or liabilities with current assets

**liquidity ratios.** Evaluate a company's ability to meet short-term cash obligations (Lenders value these ratios because they determine the borrower's ability to repay debt.)

# M

**management system.** A set of processes and procedures designed to standardize and streamline required tasks in order to increase operational efficiencies

# O

**operating expenses.** Those expenses incurred in operating a business that are usually associated with a given time period—a month, a quarter, or a year—rather than a unit of production (Also called *period costs*, operating expenses incurred in the day-to-day operation of a business are classified into four major categories: indirect construction cost, financing, sales and marketing, and general and administrative.)

**operating profit.** the profit generated from the company's own on-going operations

**overhead.** Generally includes indirect construction costs plus some or all other operating expenses

**owners' equity.** The owner's investment in a company and retained earnings (company profits the owners have chosen to reinvest in the company for growth and stability)

**owners' investment.** A component of owners' equity—capital or capital stock

# P

**payroll.** Refers to the payment of salaries and wages to company employees not payments to trade contractors

**period costs.** Another name for *operating expenses*, those expenses incurred in operating a business that are usually associated with a given time period rather than a unit of production

**posting.** The process of transferring financial transactions from all journals to specific accounts in the general ledger

**pre-acquisition costs.** Include options to purchase, engineering and architectural fees, and feasibility study expenses

**preliminary phase.** Includes all costs incurred prior to starting construction, such as architectural and engineering fees and permits

**preparation phase.** Includes cost codes associated with site clearing, excavation, and foundation

**profitability ratios.** Represent relationships among different categories in the income statement as they relate to sales or total revenues

**project.** Refers to land parcels or communities with multiple sites or to specific groups of like activities, such as remodeling projects, light commercial projects, framing, or other miscellaneous activities

**project or community income statements.** Highlight the contribution margin or operating profit that each project or community contributes to the business

**projected gross profit margin.** The gross profit margin you are planning to achieve

# R

**ratio.** The relationship between two or more numbers

**record keeping.** Recording financial transactions in the accounting system

**retained earnings.** A component of owners' equity, the accumulation of profits or losses from operations (It reflects the firm's net profit or loss accumulated from the time the business was established, less any dividends paid to the owners or cash withdrawals made by the owners.)

**return on investment.** The return received by owners and investors (It is the product of net profit, efficient use of resources, and degree of leverage.)

**revenues.** Sales made by a company, whether it is for houses, remodeling jobs, or finished lots. (They also include interest paid by banks. They represent the monetary consideration received or earned by providing goods and services to a third party.)

# S

**sales and marketing expenses.** Includes all expenses related to the marketing and selling of homes, lots, or services, including sales commissions, brochures, advertising, and signs tracked separately from costs for each home sold

**soft costs.** Generally includes indirect construction costs plus some or all other operating expenses

**subsidiary ledgers.** Accumulate data in a more detailed format for management analysis, reporting, and control (For example, the subsidiary ledgers generate job cost reports for each construction unit, job, or lot; status reports on construction loans; gross profit analysis on units sold; and other reports.)

# T

**total liabilities to owners' equity, ratio of.** Results from dividing owner's equity into liabilities

# U

**unit.** A house for the home builder, a remodeling job for the remodeler, a subdivision or community for a developer, and a commercial establishment for a light commercial builder

# V

**variable costs and expenses.** Relate directly to units built (They increase or decrease proportionately with increases or decreases in the units of production.)

**variance reports.** Compare the results of current operations with those of budgets, preceding period, and industry norms

# W

**working capital.** Current assets minus current liabilities (It measures a business's capabilities for expansion and growth.)

# Notes

**Chapter 15 Technical Aspects of Accounting**

2. Financial Accounting Standards Board (FASB), *Statement of Financial Accounting Standards No. 67* (Norwalk, CT: FASB, 1982), pgf. 4, p. 5.

3. FASB, *Statement No. 67*, pgf. 7, p. 6.

4. FASB *Statement No. 67*, pgf. 8, p. 6.

5. FASB, *Statement No. 67*, pgf. 7, p. 6.

6. FASB, *Statement No. 67*, pgf. 7, p. 6.

7. FASB, *Statement of Financial Accounting Standards No. 66,* (Norwalk, CT: FASB, 1992), pgf. 73, p. 23.

8. FASB, *Statement No. 66*, pgf. 74, p. 23.

# Index

*Page numbers for definitions are in bold.*

## ABOUT THE NATIONAL ASSOCIATION OF HOME BUILDERS

The National Association of Home Builders is a Washington-based trade association representing more than 235,000 members involved in home building, remodeling, multifamily construction, property management, trade contracting, design, housing finance, building product manufacturing, and other aspects of residential and light commercial construction. Known as "the voice of the housing industry," NAHB is affiliated with more than 800 state and local home builders associations around the country. NAHB's builder members construct about 80 percent of all new residential units, supporting one of the largest engines of economic growth in the country: housing.

 **Join the National Association of Home Builders** by joining your local home builders association. Visit www.nahb.org/join or call 800-368-5242, x0, for information on state and local associations near you. Great member benefits include

- Access to the **NAHB Collection Systems and Services** and its electronic databases, books, journals, videos, and CDs. Call 800-368-5254, x8296 or e-mail nhrc@nahb.org
- **Nation's Building News**, the weekly e-newsletter containing industry news. Visit www.nahb.org/nbn
- Extended access to **www.nahb.org** when members log in. Visit www.nahb.org/login
- **Business Management Tools** for members only that are designed to help you improve strategic planning, time management, information technology, customer service, and other ways to increase profits through effective business management. Visit www.nahb.org/biztools
- **Council membership**
    **Building Systems Council:** www.nahb.org/buildingsystems
    **Commercial Builders Council:** www.nahb.org/commercial
    **Building Systems Council's Concrete Home Building Council:** www.nahb.org/concrete
    **Multifamily Council:** www.nahb.org/multifamily
    **National Sales & Marketing Council:** www.nahb.org/nsmc
    **Remodelers Council:** www.nahb.org/remodelors
    **Women's Council:** www.nahb.org/womens
    **50+ Housing Council:** www.nahb.org/50plus

 **BuilderBooks**, the publishing arm of NAHB, publishes inspirational and educational products for the housing industry and offers a variety of books, software, brochures, and more in English and Spanish. Visit www.BuilderBooks.com or call 800-223-2665. NAHB members save at least 10% on every book.

 **BuilderBooks Digital Delivery** offers over 30 publications, forms, contracts, and checklists that are instantly delivered in electronic format to your desktop. Visit www.BuilderBooks.com and click on Digital Delivery.

 The **Member Advantage Program** offers NAHB members discounts on products and services such as computers, automobiles, payroll services, and much more. Keep more of your hard-earned revenue by cashing in on the savings today. Visit www.nahb.org/ma for a comprehensive overview of all available programs.